AFTER THE WALL

AFTER THE WALL

East Meets West in the New Berlin

JOHN BORNEMAN

BasicBooks
A Division of HarperCollins*Publishers*

Library of Congress Cataloging-in-Publication Data
Borneman, John.
    After the wall:east meets west in the new Berlin/John
Borneman.
        p. cm.
    Includes bibliographical references (p.).
    ISBN 0-465-00083-5
    1. Berlin (Germany)—History. I. Title.
DD881.B675 1990
943.1'55—dc20
                                                            90-55589
                                                                CIP

Contents

Preface

After the Wall grew out of my concern that the rush for German reunification and the euphoria in the West over the opening of the Wall, reported ad nauseum in the Western presses, would lead to a peculiar kind of political amnesia about the causes and consequences of the Cold War. In May of 1989 I had just completed a major ethnographic study about the construction of division and its effects on everyday life in the two Berlins. The revolutionary events in East Europe in 1989 demanded a new look at those divisions, from the standpoint of their collapse rather than their construction.

Most Americans experienced the events of 1989 as a blur of newspaper headlines announcing the victory of capitalism over socialism. For the citizens of East Germany, however, the Autumn Revolution of 1989 was an alternately exhilarating and tragic reality. It started with the hope of establishing popular control over the government, of restoring meaning to being East German. It ended with West Germany's virtual corporate takeover of her sister state. This takeover is far from complete, yet the terms and conditions of the new configuration, of united Berlin, are beginning to take on forms that will define the identities of future generations in a united Germany.

I hope to bring home vividly the experience of individual East Germans caught in the onslaught of this history. Through interviews with a range of Berliners East and West, I present a comprehensive and differentiated picture of the transition from socialism to capitalism. I have tried to capture experiences downplayed or overlooked altogether in the West, to examine not only the vanishing socialist society but also the nature of the Western, capitalist democracy that is to be the society of the future Germany.

Acknowledgments

First and foremost, I should like to thank the individuals, the Berliners, whose voices grace these pages. My research, like that of all anthropologists, was possible only because they trusted me and I was thus able "to write" their lives, or at least my version of them, in this book. It is drawn primarily from autobiographies gathered between fall 1986 and May 1990 while I was conducting anthropological fieldwork in the two Berlins, either recorded directly on tape or reconstructed immediately after the conversation. All personal names have been changed.

During the writing, my very talented students in Social Studies 10 at Harvard—Effie, David, Jessica, Nadine, Natalie, and Ross—were most indulgent with my preoccupation and I thank them. I also wish to acknowledge Scott Long, for without his collaboration in the final six weeks of writing it is unlikely I could have completed this book in such a short time. Dr. Long's analytical insights and editorial skills proved indispensable, immensely improving the organization, style, and logic of argument. Indeed, I must thank him for many of the felicitous expressions as well as several of the arguments in this book. All problems with the manuscript are, of course, due to my own error.

I am also grateful for the following grants and fellowships over the last three years that made my research in the two (and the new) Berlin(s) possible: Krupp Foundation; Social Science Research Council–Berlin Program for Advanced German and European Study; International Research Exchange Board; Fulbright–Hays; and the German Marshall Fund. And finally, my gratitude to the German Information Center in New York for access to their photo archive and to Martin Patek for his post-Wall photos.

1

The Many
and the One: Berlin

The city is an anagram, not of words but of lives.
—Walter Benjamin

REJOICE! THE WALL HAS FALLEN!

Surprise seized everyone when the Berlin Wall fell. Casually, in the middle of a press conference at 7:19 P.M. on the evening of 9 November 1989, Günter Schabowski, a member of the ruling Politburo of the German Democratic Republic (GDR), made the announcement. Open borders in Hungary, Czechoslovakia, and Poland had in past months facilitated a huge flight of GDR citizens to the West; Schabowski was under pressure to respond to the mass exodus, still continuing despite the newly installed, liberalizing regime. Pale but confident, Schabowski assured the world press that restrictions on visas to Western countries were in the process of being lifted, that on the following day those East Germans fleeing to West Germany through Hungary and Czechoslovakia could leave the German Democratic Republic directly without going through a third country.

Leaving the GDR would be made easy, he explained. On the next day and thereafter a simple identification at the border would be sufficient for those wanting to depart. On guard against double-talk, a journalist pounced: Did the new travel law also extend to the West Berlin border? Nervously, Schabowski wavered. He looked again at the paper containing the new regulation, given to him just minutes before. "Yes," he said, "it says here 'Berlin (West).' " Did the new law mean that any GDR citizen could, without a legal passport, travel across the border into West Berlin? Could Germans divided by 40 years of history meet, embrace, talk again? The answer was: Yes.

Within minutes several hundred young citizens had gathered expectantly outside the border crossing at Bornholmer Strasse. Rapidly other exit points filled. Within an hour a thousand people were lined up at the Chausee Strasse crossing. On the other side, Western radio and television crews awaited them, ready to capture—to create— the moment. The border guards had not been informed and were completely taken aback by the sudden crowds. Exhausted by weeks of political stress in which decades-old policies were reversed daily, overwhelmed by the mobs demanding immediate exit, and noticing Western television crews waiting on the other side, the commanding officers gave way to the masses and opened all the gates.

In the next several hours guards at all the other border crossings followed suit. Streams of Germans from both sides began gathering at the other exits, on Heinrich Heine Strasse, Invalidenstrasse, Bernauer/Eberswalderstrasse, Jannowitzbrücke, Oberbaumbrücke, Sonnenallee, Checkpoint Charlie—and, of course, at a former opening no longer functioning as an exit: the Brandenburg Gate.

Happiness filled the airwaves. Western television stations, including the popular West Berlin radio station RIAS (Radio Free Berlin), broke into their regular programming to announce the opening. In the West German Bundestag, legislators spontaneously rose and began singing the German national anthem.

Berlin was one again. The Wall had come down. On the next day, West Berlin Mayor Walter Momper declared the Germans "the happiest people in the world." Overnight a city scarred by history had become a playground, a dazed fantasyland of delight. Knuckling under to the crowds thronging the exit points, East German officials created nine more border crossings, and the East German border guards miraculously changed from the most severe to the friendliest guards in the world.

Riotous days of celebration followed. Excitement filled West Berlin, a consumer paradise of which most East Berliners had only dreamed. Apathetic West Berliners known for their dour expressions and surly manners suddenly smiled ecstatically on the street, even going so far as to give directions to lost East Berliners. Laconic bus drivers condescended to answer questions about where they were going; cab drivers gave free rides. Lavish generosity prevailed, stores gave away coffee and chocolate, movie prices were waived, bars served free drinks to their Eastern compatriots. Young and old East Germans grabbed up what they could; even Beate Uhse sex shops were opened up to whole astonished families from the GDR.[1]

RAVAGED BERLIN: HISTORY INCARNATE

The German Autumn Revolution of 1989, which had begun well before the opening of the Wall and had led to results that surprised even the participants themselves, ended in a predictable and pedestrian performance: with citizens marching to the polls on 19 March 1990 to vote. By this time there were many who felt that the revolution was governed by forces beyond the East Germans' control. Certainly it would not have been possible had Mikhail Gorbachev not attained power in the Soviet Union and unleashed a renewal process of Promethean fury. Yet "Gorbi," as the Berliners call him, had not impelled East German youth to flee across the Hungarian border or climb West German embassy fences. He had little to do with the brave people of Leipzig who demonstrated weekly during the fall of 1989, or the million demonstrators who gathered in East Berlin on 4 November to demand a true socialism and the resignation of the Politburo. These revolutionary moments reflected indigenous needs and hopes. Suspended between the giant land of *perestroika* in the East and the anxious eyes of the capitalist West, they were fully governed by neither. They were created by local German actors motivated by parochial concerns and shaped by the peculiar nature of life in a walled-in state with a capital that happened to be the half-city of Berlin.

This book might be considered a salvage operation. It attempts to recapture some of those native voices, those indigenous concerns, before they are forgotten in the coming corporate takeover of East Germany by the West, a one-sided process generally named "reunification." It attempts to rescue from historical oblivion something of the nature of everyday life in a now-vanished socialist society. It will interpret, from a social anthropological perspective, different voices from the East as they address Germany's, or more specifically, Berlin's, division and future restructuring. It is about how political structures change everyday lives and how the identities resulting from these interactions can, in turn, affect political structures.

I begin from the native's point of view, with the actual lived experiences of East Berliners at the German/German frontier, in the space where Germany is currently redefining itself. As much as possible, they speak for themselves, interrupted occasionally with questions, observations, and interpretations. What does it mean to live under socialism or capitalism? What does it mean to live with division in the context of the Cold War, and now in its aftermath with unity? What does it mean to de-Stalinize and democratize German culture? And most important, what does it mean for a state and nation to disintegrate?

I have not attempted to capture the entire Berlin experience, an abstract and largely fictive construct which would hardly lend itself to a narrative summary. Rather I have chosen, focusing on those immediately affected by the Autumn Revolution of 1989, to convey the specificity and diversity of individual lives at this crucial time in history, to portray more their range and uniqueness than their typicality and universality.

To be in Berlin, East or West, is to feel oneself in some way central. Berlin now lies gratuitously in the center of a new "common European house," to borrow the words of

Gorbachev. Reconstruction of this house will be the project of the next decade, if not the next century, for its residents. Berlin, containing both East and West, is now very much center stage, the Ur-metropole—mother to a new European polis.

Perhaps it is this quality, its total dependence on context for meaning, that qualifies it as the first postmodern city. If, as the great pre-war critic of Berlin culture, Walter Benjamin, says, Paris was the capital of the nineteenth century, Berlin is arguably the twentieth century's paradigmatic space—every major social upheaval of significance in this century has either graced or scarred its surface. Wandering along its wide boulevards and tree-lined avenues, beholding its bullet-scarred apartment facades set in relief by postmodern facelifts, I am always struck by how much history I see: not the history of other centuries preserved as in a museum, but twentieth-century history. Berlin forces one to "be there"—*Dasein*. The romanticism of Paris or the nostalgia of Vienna protect one, by contrast, from the vertigo and the peculiar imprisonment of raw, undigested present time.

If Hitler was responsible for destroying the old order of Europe, as Sebastian Haffner[2] writes, then Stalin was the architect of Europe's Cold War division. What Hitler and Stalin wrought—now receding into the distance for much of Western Europe and America, obsessed as they are by global environmental and internal economic concerns—is an ever-present problem for Germans living in the East. Only now, 45 years after the war, do they have the opportunity to deal with these albatrosses of the past as present subjects in history.

Yet this opportunity has not been widely perceived as such, and here we confront the first contradiction in the

East German experience. The initial response of most East Germans to the opening of the Wall—a meeting with the Other that was a resurrection of the repressed past—was not challenge but flight, away from murderous pasts and uncertain futures into a consumer's fleeting and slightly drunken present. It is as though the pressure of *Dasein*, of history made vivid, of responsibility, were too much. Since the Wall opened the East Germans have continually evaded the consequences of that historic rupture, and instead have sought refuge in idealized hopes and incessant shopping sprees.

The Germans have been involved in two mass movements in the last 50 years. Between 1944 and 1948, as Eastern Europe denazified itself, authorities "transferred" 6 million Germans out of Poland, 3 million out of Czechoslovakia, and several hundred thousand out of Hungary, Rumania, and Yugoslavia.[3] The present East German flight to West Germany involves approximately seven hundred thousand. We can add yet a third movement, that of 17 million East Germans to annexation. These three migrations reflect the weight of the past on the present: flight from the legacies of Hitler and Stalin.

The significance of these events has not escaped East Berlin artists. In January 1990 I saw plays in Berlin and Potsdam by two of the most respected East German playwrights, Volker Braun and Ulrich Plenzdorf. Both dramas reached their climax in scenes of anal penetration. (Given the prominence of the ass as symbol in German culture, sodomy is understood as a particularly offensive yet expected assault.) In Braun's *Transit Europa*, a sword-laden Stalin and a Hitler in Austrian lederhosen dance a *pas de deux*, each in turn bending over to be sodomized by the other. In Ulrich Plenzdorf's *Der Tag zieht den Jahrhunder-*

7

tweg (In One Day the Whole Country Unveils Itself), a Christ figure is sodomized by a corrupt general. For these East German artists predictable humiliation is the order of the day.

The West, though experienced by the defeated East Germans as a source of humiliation, also seems to promise relief. Once in the West, a higher standard of living for the two-thirds who are expected to "make it" will ameliorate, to some extent, preoccupation with origins and history, and for many it may be a viable long-term strategy. Capitalism does keep people occupied. Its busy rituals of getting and spending can repress the troubling reflective moment that follows upon remembering. To surrender control to the capitalist state and structures and thus abandon autonomy can be a panacea, offering as it does a convenient amnesia and the promise of irresponsible oblivion.

The very history of Berlin since the War has been a history practiced upon, not by, the Berliners. It is a history of names and structures imposed, of oppositions articulated, by occupation forces. It is a history in which the Berliners have continually suffered the indignity of being spoken for. On 1 May 1945, when the Soviet Army at last conquered Berlin, it was still the capital city of the Third Reich, the *Reichshauptstadt*. Fierce house-to-house fighting had reduced the city to a field of rubble, colloquially dubbed *Reichstrümmerstadt*. Three months later, the Americans traded their captured territories in Thuringia and Saxony for the western part of Berlin and moved in to occupy it (as the British and French occupied their zones). The Western-controlled districts of Berlin, particularly Dahlem, Grunewald, and Charlottenburg in the American zone, were historically by far the wealthiest. The Soviet-controlled zone was poorer, but included more industry

and the former center of the city. By 1947, differences between the Soviets and the Americans led the three zones
in the West to unite against the Soviets. With the intro-
duction in 1948 of a separate currency in the West, the four
zones were effectively reduced to two administrative units,
West and East. Since 1949, East Berlin has been the capital
of the GDR, though still officially "protected by the Soviets," while over the years West Berlin has essentially been
incorporated into the Federal Republic, though also still
under the official protection of the Americans, British, and
French. The construction in 1961 of the Wall dividing East
and West Berlin reified the division and created new ones.

The spatial division of Berlin into an "East" and a "West"
was simultaneously mapped onto the whole continent, divided by the Yalta agreement signed in 1944 by Joseph Stalin (U.S.S.R.), Winston Churchill (U.K.), and Franklin
Roosevelt (U.S.). This European phenomenon was in turn
reflected in divisions throughout the world, so that events
in Israel or Angola could only assume their full meaning in
terms of "East" and "West" and their respective interests.
And, however or wherever the pattern of events evolved,
Berlin was always central to it.

To Anglo-American eyes, the German Democratic Republic has always seemed an archetype of the Leninist, totalitarian state. Because this demonic image was so
pervasively shared, so available to Americans through film,
TV, and potted textbook histories, American politicians
could effectively wage the Cold War with uncritical public
support. Berlin became one with the Alamo and the Maine
as a memorable rallying cry, a passive symbol of endangered freedom. That is why nearly every postwar/post-Wall
president, from John F. Kennedy to Ronald Reagan, has
visited the Berlin Wall: to affirm his opposition to what was

on the other side of that "Iron Curtain." Opposition to East-bloc communism and everything associated with it confirmed and strengthened the Western commitment to the values of freedom of opinion and assembly. (It also had the practical, material function of solidifying the support of the American public for incessant rounds of arms buildup.)

Berlin, in its divided state, was useful to all parties. The Wall was a symbol, and its fall marked the collapse of a symbolic system. The opening of the Wall was a great chiasmus, a *peripateia*, a classic moment of reversal, changing the look of things and established discourses almost beyond recognition. The East-West division will never be so neat, so clean, so regularized, again. Dictators and democrats will no longer be so easy to classify.

MITTELEUROPA REDEFINED

Beneath the rigorous opposing forces that have governed a colonized and occupied Europe on both sides since 1945, there have always been alternative voices. These voices, not content with being simply denizens of an Eastern or a Western bloc, have sought to articulate their Europeanness, their ambiguous identity. The Autumn Revolution— against political divisions caused as much by the West's defensive self-definitions as by the paranoia of the East— drew largely on these long-standing alternative visions of Europe. It is worthwhile examining some of these visions.

In the early 1980s, intellectuals from Czechoslovakia, Poland, and Hungary anticipated the current intellectual ferment provoked by the end of the Cold War. The discussion centered, appropriately enough, around the naming and subdividing of the continent: Were East and West the only Europes imaginable? Was there such a thing as Central Europe, dependent on both but a part of neither? In particular, the Yalta division was eloquently challenged in the early 1980s by writers such as the Czech Milan Kundera, the Pole Czeslaw Milosz, and the Hungarian Georgy Konrad. In Jacques Rupnik's words, these writers saw as their purpose persuading their nations "to think of themselves as subjects, not merely objects, of history."[4] The subjectivity they sought to reconstruct (particularly Kundera, writing in his Parisian exile) was an identity as Central European, with less rigid state boundaries, multicultural territories, and above all, freedom from Russian domination.

At that time any alternative seemed superior to the bipolar territorial division of Europe into an "East" and a "West." Yet creation of a *Mitteleuropa,* a construct that had last been viable in the Hapsburg twilight of the nineteenth-century *fin de siècle,* was hardly an ideal solution to the region's problems. As Tony Judt remarks, it harkens back to "a region of enduring ethnic and religious intolerance, marked by bitter quarrels, murderous wars, and frequent slaughter on a scale ranging from pogrom to genocide."[5]

Given the rapidity of change in the Soviet bloc and the quickened pace of German reunification, the prospects for a romantic return to a Central European cultural unit seem highly unlikely, if ever desirable in the first place. The political systems of the world cannot be separated from cultural developments, and the culture of the old Central Europe has taken new forms since the Second World War, partly because of changes in industrial production, but also because of radically different appropriations of socialist or capitalist ideologies by the indigenous cultures. To give but one extreme example, Polish anarchism—an intense cultural resistance to forms of discipline—has, in its mixture with socialist command systems, resulted in a quite different hybrid than has the tradition of Prussian submissiveness and orderliness in East Germany. The Poles, East Germans, Czechs, Hungarians, Austrians, Bulgarians, and Rumanians are simply not the same peoples they were in 1945—nor are the Swedes, West Germans, French, Dutch, and Danes.

Moreover, integral parts of the former population are missing from the world of *Mitteleuropa*: the Central European intelligentsia and the Jews. Both groups experienced a kind of historical renaissance after the turn of the century, contributing to the unique cultural self-realizations of their countries before the 1930s. Both were ultimately decimated by the war.

Most intellectual mandarins fled into exile during the war, and after the war returned to a barren cultural landscape, nowhere more depleted than in Germany, where they were perceived, and perceived themselves, as profoundly out of place. The Jews were exterminated. "Central Europe" as a coherent topos, in its political, geographical, and literary forms, began dying with Hitler's ascension to power. What culture survived Hitler was extirpated by Stalin; what has replaced it is something of a totally different order.

As opposed to a vague trans-national, culturally based idea of *Mitteleuropa*, nationalism has proven a much more viable and unifying form of expression. The creation of a sense of nation—what we might call Germanness—is the major impetus behind the present enlargement and restructuring of the German state. It involves the expression of cultural unity in a directly, intelligibly political form. The international community understands German reunification to mean the bringing together of the divided German nation under a single state, creating what we refer to as a "nation-state."

The contemporary world is divided into such units, based on the supposition that nations are best organized and regulated when represented by a legitimate state apparatus. Yet this particular view of the world system is in fact less than 100 years old. It differs radically from the historic terms with which German intellectuals long defined their nation. Unlike Anglo-Americans, Germans have two separate concepts of the single term "nation-state." As late as 1906, the German historian Friedrich Meinecke formulated the distinction between *Kulturnation* and *Staatsnation*,[6] between a nation based on shared cultural characteristics on the one hand and one based on territorial unity with political representation in a state on the other. All those who are German by culture (members of the *Kulturnation*) do not live within the same German state (*Staatsnation*), but are spread out in many other states, with large populations in the Soviet Union, Hungary, Rumania, and Poland. Any state may contain within its borders different cultural nations. The West German state, however, has always considered itself the protector and representative of all cultural Germans, including those in East Germany, and not as a state that contains many cultures.

The old central Europe, where the German culture was in many ways the dominant one, was characterized by the overlap of boundaries between cultural groups and states. Franz Kafka, for example, was a Czech Jew who lived in Prague most of his life, but wrote in German. The prewar political unit, the German Reich, contained many non-

German areas, especially in Prussia, where Poles and Germans lived together. Poles who were juridically "German" were a common phenomenon before Nazi rule, and were often (forcibly) incorporated into German culture during the Third Reich.

The race-based concept of *Blut und Boden*, which became a Nazi rallying cry, was first widely propagated among Germans in the early years of this century. German intellectuals, from the late eighteenth century on, thought in terms of the German *Volk*, defined by particular moral, physical, or cultural traits. Throughout the eighteenth and much of the nineteenth centuries, appeals to this community were neither mystical nor racial but cosmopolitan. Kant, for example, declared in his *Anthropologie* in 1789 that Germans were without national pride and lacked passionate attachment to their fatherland.

The ethnologist and philosopher Johann Gottfried Herder, writing at the same time as Kant, expressed this view forcefully. For Herder, German history was the history "of the German nation, its constitution, ways, and language," not that of "political machines."[7] His was ethnohistory, whereby each national community had (was created by) its own culture and history, a generous view in which no culture or community was intrinsically superior to another.

Western thought since the late nineteenth century has seen the state as the natural and final expression of the nation, and has recognized nationhood only as a sort of collective mental outlook necessarily preliminary to the formation of the state. The propagators of this concept have preferred the arguments of Leopold von Ranke,[8] who maintained that although the state and the *Volk* are not identical, the will of the people can only be articulated by the state. Hence the history of the state (changes in regimes, statesmen, and policies) becomes prior, synecdochic, and superior to the history of the people. People have come to view their will as significant only when expressed by what they are told is a "natural" political entity, the state, and to see their history as attempts to build this political unity. States, in particular the Nazi state and the Federal Republic, have sought to ground the essence of their community in "nature" (biology or genes) rather than in culture.

The position of West Germany on the relation of the nation to the state, written into the constitution (Basic Law) of 1949, has always been simple: There is only one German nation into which one is born (with minor exceptions) and this nation needs and has only one legitimate state, the Federal Republic. East German leaders had a more difficult time with the concept of a German nation, for they claimed an identity based primarily on internationalist, socialist ideology. For the first 25 years of the state's existence, East German leaders argued for a Germany ultimately reunited, but only under a socialist system. Article 8 of the 1968 Constitution added recognition of "two German states" with equal rights. The leadership changed the Constitution in 1974, however, omitting Article 1 of the 1949 Constitution, which declared a "socialist state of the German nation," and replacing it with references to a "*Volk* of the German Democratic Republic," consisting of "a socialist state of workers and farmers." The ruling Socialist Unity party thus rejected all connections with German nation-ness within a single German state, preferring to re-imagine themselves as cultural Germans inhabiting a socialist state.

By the mid-1980s, the leadership had reversed itself, reclaiming elements of German history, in particular Frederick the Great and the Prussian tradition, as their own. Their efforts to legitimate themselves by grounding the state in national identity came too late, however. In 1989, the GDR simply dissolved.

The West German version of a nation triumphed and emerged from the vicissitudes of 1945–1989, prevailing even over the most basic divisions of the Cold War era. In the near future, East German territory will be annexed by the West German state; its residents will become subject to the West German Basic Law of 1949 and the German *Kulturnation* will be united in a single *Staatsnation*. This represents both a beginning and an end. It inaugurates a new attempt at asserting, on a multiplicity of levels—cultural, juridical, racial—what it means to be a German and what is entailed in the expression of the popular will by the state. And it marks the end of the separate East German attempt at self-articulation, in which socialism and nationalism moved in uneasy, imperfect, and inadequate tandem. One of the projects of this book is to examine this collapse and this regeneration, considering their causes and consequences in the integuments of individual East German lives.

THE PEOPLE SPEAK, INDIVIDUAL, ATYPICAL

Informed by three years of ethnographic fieldwork, this book seeks to illuminate the forms of sensibility, categories of thought, and schemas of action peculiar to East German residents in the city of Berlin at a particular time in history.[9] East German society, which for 40 years had its own set of norms and mores, is vanishing overnight, losing both the ideological base (socialism) of its "national identity" and the territorial sovereignty that makes it a state. It is in the context of this headlong rush to oblivion that I wish to consider it, confident that such a labor is truly postmodern in its very fragility and evanescence, for what is the essential work of thought in an era erected on destruction but the curious business of taking snapshots of disappearances?

The reader may need something to cling to as he contemplates the blur of change. I offer, therefore, a thumbnail sketch of five basic distinctive features of everyday life under "actually existing socialism," as it was officially called, in East Germany and contrast these with features of life in the West. These inform and structure this study, offering a cursory notion of what the experience of socialism was like and what is likely to supersede it.

First, time in East Berlin moved at a pace artificially slowed and petrified by both state and social structures; by contrast, time in the West moved (and moves) at a pace artificially quickened by the apparatus of capitalism.

Second, in the East fear emerged as the major regulatory factor of everyday life; in the West, the creation of specialized needs through the market apparatus regulated private experience.

Third, the East displayed a consistent colonization of public space (increased use of "instrumental rationality" or means-end calculations by the discourses and propaganda of the state), while private space was left a free zone for dreaming. In the West, public space was the zone of officially endorsed "freedom" and self-realization, while private space was consistently invaded by devices of publicity, advertising, and need-creation.[10]

Fourth, consistent with the freedom accorded private reflections in the East, a romanticism (idealized attachment

to something unattainable) and a recourse to fantasy distin-
guished the citizens' response to their own lives and to the
discourses of the state.

Fifth, "lack" and nonfocalized needs based on desire created by deprivation characterized the East whereas the
"territorialization of needs" based on desire that shifts from
object to object through the continual availability (and re-
placeability) of goods characterized the West.[11]

I hope to show these features of the experience of socialism as they play themselves out on the landscapes of
individual lives. Different points of view will appear in this
study. They will not add up to a consistent overview or to
some "average" or collective standpoint. The "average person" (genderless, classless, ageless) depicted in much social
science literature does not empirically exist, but is always
extrapolated from "real data" by some form of scientific
cunning. Anthropologists in particular have a long tradition
of looking for the average or typical when describing their
"tribe" or "folk," of sacrificing the diversity of everyday life
for a theoretically inspired pursuit of the classical and the
banal. Hence the use of the singular: Franz Boas studied
"the Kwakiutl," Bronislaw Malinowski "the Trobriander,"
Margaret Mead "the Samoan," and E. E. Evans-Pritchard
"the Nuer," to name but four of the most renowned. And
back at the academy, sitting in their well endowed chairs,
anthropologists take the name of the studied peoples, becoming Melanesianists or Polynesianists, Asianists or Afri-
canists.

I could make my own claim: *Ich bin ein Berliner,* I was
there. Yet I prefer to be both less ruthless in reducing the
complexity of separate lives to single categories and less
forward in asserting the primacy of my own insights. The
Many must claim primacy over the One, even when the

One is (in large part) oneself. I cannot generalize these experiences into an artificial unity imposed by myself; they must remain a set of statements by individual Berliners. In order to describe in the plural, in context, and in history, one must pay more attention to the exceptional than to typical lives, for only in the exceptional does one find the range of possibilities within the group. Thus I have chosen to portray individual lives of different generations, rare instances of crystallized meaning indicating how large scale political processes interact with personal histories and identities. Modern ethnographic fieldwork, which involves living over a substantial period of time with the people one studies and then focuses on the particular details of individual experience in historical context, is peculiarly suited to the task of linking the political and the personal.[12]

But what was the political dimension that informed the personal? What history did these people live through? We now turn to a summary of the events of the Autumn Revolution.

2

The Autumn
Revolution of 1989

> *The recent past always presents itself as if destroyed*
> *by catastrophes.*
> —T. W. Adorno, *Minima Moralia*

OUT OF CONTROL

The Autumn Revolution began, so far as one can date such
things, on 8 August 1989 in the city of Schlagbaum on the
Hungarian-Austrian border. About 500 East Germans took
advantage of a local fair where Hungarians and Austrians
were celebrating the dismantling of their border, to flee to
Austria. Hungarian border guards even assisted them in
their flight. Vacationing East German youths were soon
flocking to the border, crossing at night through the rolling

hills. Some planned the escape, others went along to say goodbye to friends—and ended up joining them. They were formally greeted by the Austrian government and sent on by bus to automatic citizenship and social welfare payments in West Germany. The trickle turned into a flood; thousands poured over daily. World television networks were waiting for them.

The East German government eventually convinced the Hungarians to control the border again, but this was obviously only a stopgap. How could another state be asked to control the behavior of East Germans abroad? Were they supposed to shoot if GDR citizens crossed the border?

The East Germans were under enormous pressure to regain control. At the end of September, GDR Foreign Minister Oskar Fischer announced that by 7 October—the 40th anniversary of the GDR—the whole world would see a stabilized situation in East Germany. This anniversary was to crown the 17-year rule of head of state and party Erich Honecker. All East-bloc leaders, including Gorbachev, would attend.

Meanwhile, East Germans were seeking other avenues of escape, taking refuge in West German embassies in Budapest, Prague, and Warsaw. Two weeks before the anniversary, in an ostentatious show of forgiveness, all the embassy-imprisoned refugees were officially allowed egress to the West.

The state's proffered carrot concealed a stick for those left at home. Honecker also issued a command for the "Maintenance of Security and Order." Anticipating protests at the celebration, the edict ordered security forces to crack down on demonstrators, even to shoot if necessary. This prospect later came to be known—and feared—within the GDR as a "China Solution," after the massacre in Peking, China, of student demonstrators in Tiananmen Square in April 1989, an event the GDR leadership officially applauded.

Protests occurred nonetheless: At the state-sponsored rallies and anniversary parades, crowds chanted "Gorbi, help us" and "Glasnost and Perestroika." The appeal to the model of Soviet liberalization was a peculiarly effective assault on the will of the old leadership. The GDR had long proclaimed itself "bound in perpetual socialist brotherhood"; its moral and psychological dependence on Moscow was greater than the leadership was willing to admit publicly. Yet ever since Gorbachev came to power, the GDR had taken great pains (and impaled itself on formidable contradictions) to distance itself from Soviet reforms. Kurt Hager, Honecker's chief ideologist, claimed in 1987 that each socialist country could now build its own type of socialism, that "just because your neighbor wallpapers his home anew does not mean that you have to." (This earned him the nickname *Tapeten-Kurt*, Wallpaper Kurt.)

Gorbachev himself apparently warned Honecker in a private meeting that "Life will punish those who come too late to history." But his advice to Honecker was too late. Events began to take on a breakneck momentum of their own.

The police and Stasi (state security) worked together to avenge the public humiliation of the leadership. Scenes of violent confrontation stained the streets of East Berlin, Dresden, Karl-Marx-Stadt, Plauen, Leipzig, and Magdeburg as the state cracked down on demonstrators. A deluge of press accounts labeled the participants rowdies and *"Provokateure."* The official Socialist Unity party (SED) newspaper *Neues Deutschland* claimed that the Berlin demonstration on the evening of the state's birthday party included organized attacks on the people's police. The *Volkspolizei* reported fifty-seven of their ranks injured and two unable to resume work. They had justifiably defended themselves against the mob, they maintained, and "mob leaders" were taken into custody.

Within two weeks after the "attacks," eighty-three people had complained to the State Prosecuting Attorney of damages inflicted by the Stasi, police, and other security forces. Reports by those who had been taken into custody (1,047 citizens had been arrested) did not corroborate the state's accounts. Many so-called "rowdies" were innocent teenagers on their way home from school, housewives returning from work, or indeed any pedestrians in the vicinity.

Much of the battle was staged around the Gethsemanekirche in the Prenzlauer Berg section of Berlin. The churches opened their doors to the demonstrators, but the Stasi awaited them if they wandered back out onto the street. If caught, they were subjected to twenty-four hours of what citizens soon dubbed "neo-Nazi interrogations." Those arrested were often beaten without provocation. Once in the police station, most of them were immediately photographed, fingerprinted, and booked on trumped-up charges. Many were made to stand for hours with their faces to the wall, legs spread apart, some half-naked or fully unclothed, in mostly unheated rooms. They were periodically taken for interrogation and were forced to sign fabricated protocols of the events.

Citizens called for an immediate investigation of police conduct. The commission eventually appointed to investigate the events viewed videos of the demonstrators taken by the Stasi. General-Major Dr. Haehnel of the Stasi spoke before the commission, insisting that demonstrators provoked the police to violence. The videos showed a different story. In one example from the commission report, a demonstrator was sentenced to six months imprisonment for calling "No Violence" about fifteen times. His pleas, the Stasi argued, were intended to provoke the police to attack.

Through word-of-mouth and Western television, the extent of police brutality quickly became known. The credibility of a regime willing to inflict such savagery on its citizens with the left hand, while anointing and garlanding itself with the right, was irreparably lost.

A PEOPLE ON THE MARCH

From Berlin the focus of events switched to Leipzig. Since early September, spontaneous Monday demonstrations had become part of the weekly routine in Leipzig. Despite word of police brutality in Berlin, 50,000 brave demonstrators took to the streets on 9 October in a decisive show of strength that broke the regime's will. Not since 17 June 1953, when workers thronged the streets in protest, bringing Soviet troops to East Berlin to quell the riots, had there been so much "people power" on the streets.

The regime had been readying its forces for a deterrent bloodbath, and the weekly Leipzig demonstration was to be the place. The SED newspaper *Leipziger Volkszeitung* threatened on the Friday before that "counterrevolutionary actions must be finally and effectively stopped—if need be, with weapons in our hand!" Stasi units were instructed to fire on the demonstrators. Blood banks in local hospitals had been filled, and medical staff put on alert. But the confrontation took an unusual turn.

Around two in the afternoon of 9 October, Stasi agents

(plainclothes as usual, but identifiable nonetheless) began gathering in pairs outside the Nikolaikirche, where a peace mass was to begin at five. At three, in a pompous display of state power, columns of police vans with uniformed people's police began circling the central squares of Leipzig, finally halting on side streets. The people began filing into the church. At four-thirty, church officials hung a sign over the window on the entrance to the Nikolaikirche: "closed because overfull." Even the standing places in the back were taken. Crowds massed outside the church, soon thickening to more than 10,000. At six, the three thousand people in the church began to leave, joining a crowd outside that had grown to 20,000. Silently, slowly, the crowd, by now 50,000 strong, marched to the Platz der Republic before the Leipzig train station. The demonstration drew people from every class and milieu, every age group and political persuasion. Demonstrators alternately chanted: "Gorbi, Gorbi!" "We Are The People, We Are The People!" "Freedom, Equality, Liberty!" "New Forum, New Forum!" "No Violence, No Violence!"

As the Stasi waited for the final attack orders, prominently placed loudspeakers along the march route began to broadcast an extraordinary appeal. Kurt Masur, the world renowned conductor of the Gewandhaus Orchestra, with the performer Bernd Lutz Lange from the Leipzig cabaret "Akademixern," Peter Zimmermann, priest and member of the Christian Democrat Union (CDU) board of directors, and three high-level Leipzig SED functionaries addressed the two sides:

Today we are brought together by our sense of common concern and responsibility. We are apprehensive about the development in our city and are seeking a solution. We all need a free exchange of opinion about the further development of socialism in our land. Therefore the undersigned promise to all citizens that they will use their entire strength and authority for this purpose, and that this dialogue will take place not only in the district of Leipzig, but also with our regime. We ask you to act with prudence so that a peaceful dialogue will be possible.

The demonstrators slowly disbanded. The police and security forces did not attack. Whether it was the size of the crowds, the moral authority of the people's silent commitment to nonviolence, or the solemn appeal of Masur et al., that dissuaded local Stasi authorities from charging the crowds, their guns remained silent. The oppressor's nerve had been broken.

The state's terror apparatus had at long last broken down. No longer able to rely on the Stasi to apply and enforce a "China solution," the leadership took two days to respond to their failure of will. On Tuesday the ruling gerontocracy met among themselves; on Wednesday they called in all the SED district leaders. That evening, through their central propaganda instrument, the evening news program *Aktuelle Kamera*, they took their stand on the recent events. They issued a 15-minute appeal for solidarity and unity among socialists, and for collective resistance to the evil imperialists in the Federal Republic of Germany (FRG). They made a few references to their willingness to engage in a dialogue and expressed eagerness to hear different suggestions for building an attractive socialism. Yet no serious self-criticism was expressed.

A REGIME TOPPLES

Honecker had never expected this. Much as Hitler imagined himself sole owner and proprietor of a thousand-year Reich, Honecker seems to have supposed the system he presided over could endure defiantly regardless of what happened in the West or in the Soviet Union. Only months before, he had asserted in a well-publicized interview that the Wall would stand for at least another hundred years. Yet the regime's brutal behavior during the first days of protests had proven that it could only legitimate itself through force. Now, with Gorbachev and the Soviet army no longer willing to prop up East German power, and with the government unable to rely on the secret police, Honecker's days were numbered.

Illness perhaps added to his troubles. The seventy-seven-year-old leader had been sick much of the summer and Berlin was full of rumors about his ebbing strength. Initiating one humorous exchange between East and West in September, the scandal-mongering West German newspaper *Bild*, owned by the right-wing publisher Springer Verlag, ran a huge headline covering the entire front page, announcing "Honecker lies dying." The next day an editorial signed E. H. appeared in *Neues Deutschland*, the official Communist party newspaper, decrying the rumor and attacking West Germany. The following day, *Bild*'s headline, again covering the entire front page, read: "Honecker reads *Bild*."

Honecker's regime lurched on for a few more days, but the events of 9 October had undone it. On 18 October, the Central Committee voted to replace him with Egon Krenz, whom Honecker had designated as his crown prince. The other two hard-liners in the Central Committee, Joachim

Hermann, responsible for the media, and Günter Mittag, in charge of the economy, were also forced to resign.

Krenz and most of the rest of the leadership promptly jumped on the reform bandwagon, at least in their public utterances. On his first day in office, Krenz visited workers in the Seventh of October Machine-Tool Factory in East Berlin, then drove to a hunting lodge just outside the city to meet leaders of the Protestant church, seeking out groups central to the opposition who might legitimate, and save, him. Before the end of the month he flew to Moscow to cloak himself in Gorbachev's mantle—all to no avail.

Throughout October citizens throughout the GDR met with public officials in town meetings. The leitmotif of the leadership's new love song to the people became *Dialog-bereitschaft*, readiness to engage in dialogue. In Berlin, the Union of Writers, the Union of Artists, and the national association of lawyers organized public discussions, as did Kurt Masur and his Gewandhaus Orchestra in Leipzig. The discussions intensified rather than pacified public discontent, however. Giving voice to years of accumulated dissatisfaction, they brought to the fore more and more demands which the regime could not or would not meet. Dialogue was not enough for the aroused citizenry. They kept raising the stakes, calling for immediate, ever more substantive changes, not merely a paternal regime with an attentive ear.

The Monday demonstrations in Leipzig continued to grow in size. On 9 October approximately 70,000 had demonstrated; on 16 October 120,000, on 23 October 300,000, on 30 October nearly half a million. Demonstrators carried posters proclaiming "New Politics with the Old Crowd," "Stasi Out," "Put the Stasi to Work," and "Legalize New

Forum" (New Forum was the underground opposition movement that the government still refused to recognize).

In these heady days of revolutionary spirit, the demonstrators retained a biting sense of humor. During the fortieth anniversary celebration, the regime had flooded the stores in the republic with bananas, rarely available before. One popular banner now read: "Don't Fill Our Mouth With Talk Of Reform And Try To Shut Us Up With Bananas." In these mid-October demonstrations the people began chanting "We Are The People," and "We're Staying Here", a provocation to the regime and an angry stab at the many who had fled the troubled GDR.

With Krenz's ascension, the media began to take up previously taboo questions, such as economic problems and political corruption, further arousing discontent. On 30 October GDR television reported the Monday Leipzig demonstration live. On the following Thursday massive, unplanned, and uncoordinated protests and demonstrations spread like wildfire throughout the republic: 10,000 people demonstrated in Gera, 30,000 in Erfurt, 10,000 in Halle, 15,000 in Guben. More heads rolled. By 2 November seven more members of the Politburo had resigned.

Three social groups moved into the leadership vacuum left by the incapacitated state: artists, Lutheran ministers, and lawyers. Although these groups were primarily responsible for organizing and guiding the masses against the state on 4 November and thereafter, others flocked around them.

HARD-WON, SHORT-LIVED DEMOCRACY

The nation's resentment found its ultimate public expression on 4 November in East Berlin. An estimated one million people gathered from all parts of the republic for the first demonstration in Alexanderplatz not organized by the state—a demonstration televised in both Germanies. It was initially conceived as a march through the city to a final gathering at Platz der Akademie, and planned for either 4 or 19 November. But (in an ominous foreshadowing of future relations between the two republics) the West German media forced the East's hand: the *Tageszeitung* in West Berlin listed it as taking place on 4 November, compelling the organizers to settle on the earlier date.

The revolutionary spirit of 4 November is most directly evident in the spontaneous banners and posters that dotted the demonstration, brought by people of all sorts—small groups of students, work brigades, dramatists, independent women, university teachers, writers, independent trade unionists, newly formed political parties, handicapped people in wheelchairs, environmentalists. The demonstration was huge and lively, yet quiet and generous at the same time, a protest against the dying regime and a rally celebrating East Germans as a group, as a *Volk* with a 40-year history. Most posters demanded a radical change in the power structure and free political assembly. Among the thousands of signs carried, not a single one pleaded for unification. It was the first real expression of the unity of the nation. Unbeknownst to its participants, it was also a last attempt at establishing a separate East German identity.

People began gathering at five in the evening and the festivities lasted until two the next morning. As citizens came from all over the republic, the trains to Berlin were filled; in some cities, tickets had been sold out early in the week. Twenty-six speakers championed reform, all speaking for a better, more humane socialism. Establishing the legality of the state was the overriding theme. Gregor Gysi, head of the GDR Union of Jurists and soon to be leader of a reorganized Communist party, proclaimed: "The best state security is legal security." Günter Schabowski, the former Berlin SED leader turned reformer, claimed "We are learning indefatigably." Because he belonged to the current leadership, he was the only speaker to be booed.

Most of the speakers insisted that the revolution had only just begun, that the people must carry on to make it irreversible. Novelist and playwright Christoph Hein described the present society as one having "little to do with socialism; rather, it is a society marked by bureaucracy, demagogy, spying, illegal use of power, infantilization of the population, and criminality." Writer Stefan Heym, often called "the leader of the revolution" by the West Germans, argued for "a socialism—not the Stalinist one, but the right one—which we can finally build, for our use and for the use of all of Germany. This socialism is unthinkable without democracy." Christa Wolf urged "democracy, now or never." She cited a banner, "a suggestion for the first of May [demonstration]: the leadership marches in front of the people."

The Germans—who, Lenin once complained, would never storm a railway station without first buying a ticket— had taken to the streets and, quietly, without self-proclaimed leaders, without a promise of assistance from their capitalist neighbors, staged a revolution from the bottom up. It was a democratic revolution, the first in Germany since 1918, for the West Germans had had their democracy forced on them by the Americans, much as prosperity had been spoon-fed them by the Marshall Plan. The East Germans were winning democracy for themselves, grasping their own power of self-determination. Little did they know on 4 November 1989 that their victory was to last five days.

THE RACE DOWNHILL

The opening of the Wall, on 9 November 1989, freed East Germans to visit their rich kin in the West. Who could have foreseen the reaction of East Germans, after 28 years of "containment," to West German abundance? On their visits to West Berlin in the following days they were overwhelmed.

After the opening of the Wall, each weekend was marked by an orgy of shopping as millions of East Germans stormed West Berlin and the border cities of West Germany. On 11 November reportedly 2 million East Germans visited West Berlin as part of a unity celebration. Many stores in West Berlin and West Germany, which legally must close by 6:00 P.M., stayed open until they ran out of buyers. The official exchange rate for Eastmarks in West German banks quickly adjusted itself from seven to one to ten to one. The unofficial rate often went as high as twenty to one! In the first twelve days after the opening of the Wall, East German authorities estimated that 3 billion Eastmarks were smuggled to the West. Antique shops in the East closed within a week after the opening, for owners could now smuggle their antiques to the West and sell them for deutschmarks.

Yet it wasn't the drain of money that sapped the revolution's strength. It wasn't the East Germans' fixation on bananas and exotic fruits they had never seen, their delight in new stereos and washing machines, their fascination with beautiful girls—pictured, inflatable plastic, and real—for sale, that determined the revolution's fate. It was not these evanescent emotions but the underlying disorientation such abundance produced. It was the terrifying feeling of inferiority, the sense that everything they had stood and lived for, their sacrifices and self-satisfactions alike, were worthless in the face of Western prosperity. For two years during which visa policies had been comparatively relaxed, East Germans had been trickling over the border to West Germany. Those who returned home had usually done so with a feeling of devalued selfhood, of doubt and fear, a bruised sense of having been assaulted by a superior power. Now East Germans were taking a beating not as individuals, but as a society. In response, collectively, they demanded West Germany's rich way of living for themselves.

Time speeded up drastically after the Wall fell. The East German state transformed itself with dizzying speed, but at the same time the significance of these events was radically devalued, as the state itself shrank to a triviality, a nine nanoseconds wonder. On 13 November the leadership formally rescinded the *Schiessbefehl*, the order responsible for shooting 191 people who tried to flee the GDR after 1961. The Communist party gave up its claim to exclusive power on 1 December. Such radical changes would have attracted world attention had the state not already been eclipsed by the glittering West German sun. On 3 December Krenz resigned his posts in the Politburo and Central Committee and as head of the party; three days later, he resigned as head of state—now no one remembers who Egon Krenz was. Socialism and the whole integument of GDR existence were rapidly dying.

The SED, its credibility devastated, was unable to stop the nation's steady loss of political integrity and power. The party experienced a steady membership decline from over 2.4 million in August 1989 to less than 800,000 before the elections in March 1990. Its new leaders were never able to separate themselves from the dark past of their party. Interim Prime Minister Hans Modrow, who took office on 13 November, had been an opponent of Honecker, relegated to a regional office in Dresden for his outspoken support of reform. He commanded wide respect but was condemned for not making a clean sweep of the state security system. He disastrously proposed remaking it in the image of the Office of Constitutional Protection in the Federal Republic and was forced to abandon the effort.

Nor could opposition politicians muster enough authority to prevent the West German takeover, or even to allow the nation to bargain on equal terms. The very day the Wall was opened, the writer Christa Wolf read on GDR television an appeal signed by artists and opposition group leaders, asking the people, still emigrating in droves, "to stay here with us." The appeal read:

Dear fellow citizens, women and men,

We are all deeply disturbed. We see that daily thousands are leaving our land. We know that their mistrust in the renewal of our social well-being has been reinforced by a politics that has failed us right up to the last few days. We are aware of the impotence of our words compared with mass movements, but we have no other means than our words. Those who are now still leaving deflate our hope. We ask of you, remain in your homeland, stay here by us!

What can we promise you? Nothing easy, but a useful life. No quick prosperity, but participation in great changes. We want to work for democratization, free elections, legal security, and freedom of action. One cannot overlook the fact that decade-old encrustations cannot be done away with in weeks. We stand now at the beginning of fundamental changes in our country.

Help us to construct a truly democratic society, which also preserves the vision of a democratic socialism. It is no dream, if you work with us to prevent it from again being strangled at birth. We need you. Pull yourself together and come to us, to those of us who want to remain here. Trust.

Yet there was no trust and the opposition, led by intellectuals, did not know how to create it. The authors of the appeal later accepted the endorsement of Egon Krenz, thereby losing what small support the statement had garnered. People bitterly complained that the opposition could still be blinkered by the ruses of the old guard.

Bärbel Bohley, once heralded as the Joan of Arc of the revolution, lost her following after she declared on 12 November that "The people have gone crazy and the regime has lost its senses." Free elections, she declared, would be impossible, a mere circus of irrationality, in the vortex created by the open Wall. She was roundly attacked by all political parties, including fellow members of the opposition. In retrospect, she was arguably correct, but the blithe insensitivity of her statement, implying that her immature people could only attain freedom in a protected hothouse atmosphere, was symptomatic of the opposition's remoteness from popular reality. It could not create a program attractive enough to counter the seductions of the West.

Members of the opposition, including Bohley, were invited, from December through the elections in March, to participate in round table discussions with the SED on the conduct of the elections and the structure of a new society. They were handicapped, however, by their concept of democracy as a consensus of all. The SED and those political parties with West German counterparts—primarily Social Democrats (SPD), Christian Democrats (CDU), and Liberal Democrats (LDPD) in the East (matched with Free Democrats [FDP] in the West)—operated with a concept of democracy as a struggle of interest groups, fighting to win elections to establish legitimacy to rule and implement particular programs. The round table kept up the front that the intellectuals in New Forum demanded of them, striving painfully for unanimity. On the streets and on the airwaves, however, the parties were contending for support. Members of New Forum were involved in investigative commissions and local initiatives, leaving little energy and few resources for organizing a political party from the base. The parties with West German support, in the meantime, were devoting their attention to the elections. The round table agreement that political parties would accept no assistance from "foreign" sources was almost universally disregarded. West German parties financed, dominated, and decided the East German elections.

Thus, after the opening of the Wall, the fate of East Germany became a question removed from East German control. The ragged state was delivered over to West Germany like a decapitated John the Baptist to an eager Salome. West German Chancellor Helmut Kohl issued ultimatums to the East German regime, exploiting West German economic superiority and East German moral and political uncertainty to dictate the terms of German/German relations.

Kohl's unwillingness to support an interim SED or even a coalition regime until the 18 March elections may have been understandable given the totalitarian history of the Communist party. However, he also arbitrarily expropriated the unique opportunities of the historical moment for the GDR population. He took away their right to self-determination, giving them instead a prepackaged West German self, structured around prosperity. Kohl reckoned on, and helped bring about, a complete collapse not only of the East German regime but also of East German identity and independence, after which he could integrate East Germans into West German society (and into the NATO alliance) on his own terms. The whole history of East Germany, from Hitler to Stalin to a failed socialism, was rendered supererogatory save as a mere overture to the opening of the Wall and the triumphant apocalypse of West German glory.

The failure of the East German state to inculcate or articulate a lasting identity in its citizens and the ways in which capitalism built on this failure are central to this book. To see the failure in its most immediate, most awkward manifestation, we must turn to the major event of the revolution, the moment when crisis crystallized into comedy: the opening of the Berlin Wall. How was that astonishing moment of contact with the long-dreamed-of West experienced by individual Berliners? That is the burden of the next chapter.

3

One Night in Jericho: The Wall Comes Down

Banners of scarlet, laughter, insanity, trumpets.
—Georg Trakl, *Trumpets*

"IT WAS CHAMPAGNE!"

Hildegard, forty years old, a mother, a housewife, an amateur singer, and a former teacher, was working as a bookkeeper in 1989. Before the Wall came tumbling down, she had never been to the West. Her experience of the shock of encounter is very close to the one we (the Western *we*) would like to suppose ideal, or typical. It was a giddy moment, euphoric, carnivalesque, a night she knows she'll never forget.

"I was performing with my cabaret group in Cottbus,

about three hours' drive away from Berlin, when someone said they'd heard on the radio that the Wall had been opened. We all dismissed that as rumor. But you didn't know what to believe; there were so many rumors going around, and then, on the next day, we would find out they were true! About an hour after the performance, we were driving back, and heard it on the radio ourselves. When we arrived in Berlin, we immediately drove across into West Berlin."

The first crossing was all a chaotic blur, noisy, exhausting. "The city center, on KuDamm, was one big party. After an hour we came back, and my friend from the cabaret dropped me off at my home.

"Bert, my husband, was away on a business trip and the kids were already asleep. Thirty minutes later, my friend called me back and said he couldn't sleep. I couldn't sleep either! So we decided to go back again. It was something like two or three in the morning. He picked me up and we went back to the party on KuDamm. I didn't come back till it was time for my kids to get up.

"The next weekend Bert and I and the kids took a trip to West Germany. People were passing out drinks along the freeway. There were huge lines." Hildegard's senses were disoriented in this brave new world. She expected all the goods and objects to be utterly different and saw the unusual lurking everywhere. Even the most familiar things took on an ad hoc absurdity, a strangeness specific to the occasion. "I took a glass of something and thought: what kind of funny lemonade is this? It was champagne!"

A sort of civil ellipsis had set in, a relaxation of all the forms and rules, a disorder presided over by a multiplicity of Lords of Misrule.

"That first week people were marvelous. There was an

openness, a new spirit, a generosity." Things actually worked better, in some ways, amid the mayhem. The ordinary competitiveness of German life diminished. The caste system that generally prevails on the *Autobahnen* in both East and West Germany (the only freeways in Europe without a speed limit)—the unspoken rule whereby less powerful automobiles defer to their faster cousins, so that cars like Bert and Hildegard's rattletrap East German-made Wartburg are nudged permanently into sluggish side lanes—was set aside. Hildegard remembers, "People even let you pass them on the freeway!"

"And the kids?" I asked her about her two sons, aged ten and twelve.

"We've always taken an interest in teaching the children world geography," she said. In early summer of 1989 they had applied to visit one of Bert's aunts in West Germany for her sixty-fifth birthday. Only Bert's application was approved. He could not take his family along.

Now everything was different. "My youngest, he wanted to go to Heidelberg right away. They were ready to go to West Germany on the very evening after they had heard about the opening."

A NECESSARY EVIL

Frau Erika Gruner remembers the same chaos, but less happily. Seventy-eight years old, a former judge and law professor, Frau Gruner, who was born in Berlin in the antediluvian days before the First World War, was returning from a trip to West Germany on the evening of the opening.

"I'd just arrived in Berlin on the train. It took one hour

to move from Zoologischer Garten [in West Berlin] to Friedrichstrasse [in East Berlin, a journey that usually takes fifteen minutes at most]. I knew something was up. The mood was fantastic. I had to change trains at Zoo, but there were so many people milling around the platforms that it was even difficult to get out of the train. So many colorful people, dressed in leather or with wild hairdos, types I don't automatically trust. A young man approached me and said, 'Why don't you stay here?' But I had my suitcase and it was so early in the morning."

So, almost uniquely among the thousands of East Germans on the move that night, Frau Gruner headed East, to the quiet and security of her subsidized apartment, moving against the stampeding throngs who were suddenly being told, by the radios and televisions and special editions of newspapers, that they personified History.

"There was a tremendous noise at Brandenburg Gate, which I could hear from the train as we approached Friedrichstrasse [an S-Bahn station]. When I got to Friedrichstrasse, another young man approached me and asked, 'Would you like me to carry your suitcase? I won't steal it, I promise.' Then I said, 'Okay, that would be very nice of you.' And he escorted me to my house."

I asked her if the experience had brought her to tears.

"No, it didn't. When the war came to an end—then I cried. For me that was overwhelming. The opening of the Wall was important and necessary; I agree with its destruction, and the spirit was great, but there are still so many unsolved problems. All the weaknesses of the system, primarily economic ones, which caused us to build the Wall, are still there. Nothing has gone away."

Two years before, in 1987, I had asked Frau Gruner if the building of the Wall in 1961 had changed her life.

"No," she answered. "I fully accepted the Wall. I still do today." She remembered the years before the Wall was erected, during which she'd worked as a judge on the *Kammergericht*, the highest court of appeal in East Berlin. "I lived through the plundering of our city [by West Germans]—you can't really call it anything else. And how nice the people found *that* situation! If only they could work in West Berlin and live in East Berlin so they could pay the cheap rent here."

The West German government at that time had refused to recognize the legitimacy of the East German state. Conspiring to destroy "Bolshevism," as it called the East German experiment, it passively and gleefully watched as its citizens set up black markets for East German goods and currency. These highly profitable exchanges depleted East German capital reserves, thereby making goods in the East scarce and expensive.

"I remember in a dairy in Berlin-Weissensee; there were only two people working; there wasn't enough milk for the children. That was the last straw. I wasn't shocked when they built the Wall, even though I had relatives in West Berlin. It was a question of existence here. Naturally it was very hard on those who had relatives on the other side, but that wasn't a hardship we'd created. The Wall was the consequence, not the cause."

Frau Gruner spared no criticism of the West's role in the whole postwar period. West Germany "always exploited" overtures from the GDR, she maintained. "As soon as something was a bit relaxed, they exploited us. Our good intentions in normalizing relations with West Germany came to nothing, not because our regime was intent on being malicious to its citizens, but because we were so vulnerable to the West. The border was used extensively for smuggling [subsidized goods from the East], and what could one do about that?" She saw no alternative to the Wall. "Yes, I'm convinced about that, as hard as it was for so many people."

The Wall was enabling, not enclosing, in Frau Gruner's view. In 1987, she saw it as circumscribing a hothouse in which socialism could flower in a hostile world.

"Up to now, the West has been riding on the idea of freedom, although it is based on lies. Margaret Thatcher, for example. I had to laugh when I heard her say the Soviet Union should worry about human rights. When I think about what is happening in Ireland! When the political side of socialism—democracy, I mean—finally blooms, then socialism will be a danger for capitalism. First the social security, then the unfolding of an extraordinary culture of which we can only have a presentiment . . . and add to that genuine human rights, freedom to move, the worth of every individual person. Capitalism cannot compete with that. Socialism does not need bombs or weapons to gain acceptance. [The idea] animates my every day. I am, yes, absolutely convinced that we'll make it."

One night two years later, the Wall fell, the party started, and Frau Gruner went home to bed.

"LIKE—BUT OH HOW DIFFERENT"

From the other side of the Wall, Western eyes peered at the liberated East with a variety of reactions: delight, contempt, a sort of patronizing sophistication, and, in some cases, the patient amazement of an amnesiac who painstakingly reassembles forgotten memories, as though old synapses were being stitched together in a delicate neural operation, and sensations long thought lost were becoming vivid, real, again.

This was the case with many former East Germans, who found their abandoned country suddenly accessible once more. Among them were Franziska and her mother Beate, who had received permission to emigrate to West Germany in February 1988. The opening of the Wall had special and quite different meanings for each. Beate was born 11 years before the Wall was built, Franziska 12 years after. The safety of being enclosed in a zoolike fortress protected Franziska's childhood; earlier the same fortress had frustrated and perverted Beate's youth.

Beate remembered the sudden slamming of a barrier across her city and her county in 1961. The Wall had a double impact on her. When she was finally granted permission to leave, the Wall closed behind her and cut her off from her past. In mid-November 1988, safely ensconced in West Berlin, she was planning to visit her best friend's country house back in the East. With bags full of fruit and coffee, and chocolates in hand, she stood in line at Friedrichstrasse with all the other West Berliners—only to be told "no entry," *Einreiseverbot*. She returned haggardly to her apartment that afternoon, and said to me, "I've been denied entry at the border."

I had no response. To be sure, she had come West to start over again, but she had had no idea how absolute the forgetting would have to be, how clean a slate she would be handed. There was no return.

She tried on other days, hoping the authorities had made a mistake, or perhaps would indeed make a mistake and let her back in by accident. All to no avail. She wrote several authorities, appealing for help: the FRG Ministry of the Interior, West Berlin's Mayor Momper, even Honecker himself. Her mother was sick and needed her care; couldn't something be worked out? She received no response.

A year later, Beate was awakened by a call from the friend she was to visit the first day she had been denied entry. It was one in the morning on 10 November and her friend was calling from a phone booth in West Berlin.

"Beate, the border is open. I'm here!" Beate, groggy from sleep after a 12-hour work day as chief doctor in a psychiatric clinic, was dazed and irritated by the call. The words from the other end didn't register.

"But I'm here," screamed her usually soft-voiced, self-effacing friend. Finally she persuaded Beate to get up and come see for herself. Beate threw on her clothes and went outside into the sudden wholeness.

If for Beate the opening was a miraculous reconciliation of old and new selves, which sewed her severed life back together, for Franziska it was a wonderful party. Franziska had never experienced the loss of freedom her mother felt at the building of the Wall. The Wall had been a given for Franziska. Before the family left East Germany, she had cared little about crossing a formerly open border. When she finally did cross the border, it disappeared, as it were, as if it had never been significant. Unlike her mother, Franziska was never denied permission to visit the East, to go back home. She was privileged, because she hadn't yet come of age. Hence resettling simply meant for Franziska that the Wall became infinitely permeable. She could shuttle back and forth at will. She maintained steady contact with her friends in Jena, Dresden, and East Berlin, and on the night of the opening, they all visited her. Her main reaction was happiness that her friends were calling on her for a change.

If Beate, from a middle generation, experienced the Wall

as oppressive from both sides, the generations before and after her were more accepting of the concrete monstrosity. The ease with which Franziska had come to terms with the Wall bore a certain resemblance to Frau Gruner's attitude. For both the sixteen-year-old and the septuagenarian, the bricks of the Wall had provided a haven.

Ultimately, only people of Frau Gruner's generation could live in the fortress as its architects meant it to be experienced—as a utopian protection against a cruel world. Frau Gruner had lived through the logic of the Wall. She genuinely believed the GDR needed protection from capitalist *Ausblutung*, the bleeding-dry policies of the Federal Republic. She understood self-containment as a response to the West's strategy of containing communism. It was part of the cost—temporary, she hoped—of socialist development. And, drawing on her own experience of Hitler's Germany, she associated the capitalist alternative with militarism and fascism.

Furthermore, Frau Gruner's childhood and youth oscillated between the most diverse and demanding poles of experience. On the one hand, insecurity and injustice, unemployment, political chaos, war, famine, flight, death. On the other hand, adventure and idealism, work as an antifascist in the resistance, joining in the creation of a new socialist state. She had undergone the extremes of confinement and freedom. Franziska had experienced only predictability, regularity, security, and a mild, not terribly grating containment.

Franziska's ease with the Wall turned into something very much like boredom. This side, that side—it was all the same, a vague and vertiginous round of friends and music, music and friends. Even the eventual eruption of history into Berlin's daily routine on 9 November didn't exactly add excitement. History was just another guest at the party.

A LIFE DEVALUED

Regine, a fifty-five-year-old East German filmmaker, had watched the building of the Wall as a student. Its opening was a shock and in many ways not a pleasant one. She was upset at the sudden and calamitous way that East German life lost its shape and integrity in a single loud explosion as of corked-up champagne. The aspirations for freedom the GDR citizens had nourished for months or years suddenly gave way to a frenzy of vacationing, to the ubiquitous, shockingly bourgeois ambition to spend a weekend in the West.

"Of course, it was horrible to be locked in all those years. And now we have the opportunity to travel, along with other opportunities that were closed to me before. But traveling didn't mean that much to me. I didn't go to West Berlin until several weeks after the opening. What should I do there? Run up and down KuDamm?

"To be sure, we were all overjoyed at the collapse of the regime," Regine explained. "But then it all went so fast and frenzied. For example, the opening of the border—that was not planned."

During the border festivities Regine was recovering from her first trip to West Germany in over 15 years, permitted in the first wave of relaxation as the Honecker regime fell. She lectured in Marburg on three documentary films she had made, on KZ Ravensbruck, the infamous all-female concentration camp; on Communist party leader Rosa

Luxemburg; and on the anti-Fascist painter Fritz Kramer. The trip had been trying. She was severely attacked by several among her hosts, especially by former GDR residents, for remaining in East Germany. How could she stay there, they asked? Wasn't she supporting the totalitarian system by her continued presence?

Regine had been subjected to considerable political pressure while making the films, especially the documentaries on KZ Ravensbruck and Luxemburg. The authorities wanted Communists shown as central figures, resistance fighters, and heroes, always in the right. Regine wanted to demonstrate that Communists were not the only sufferers at the hands of the Third Reich, and that Luxemburg was a radical democrat rather than a purely orthodox party member. Her West German audiences were bored by these themes. For them, the past was passé. They saw in her ideological struggles only pale echoes of ones they'd been through 20 years before. Why was she making such an issue of these stale disputes?

There was a wall between Regine and the harsh frowning faces in the tiers of seats. She couldn't translate her own experiences across the barbed wire of knitted brows, make her struggles meaningful to her hearers. The battles she'd fought in the East were insignificant to the confident West Germans. Her life, she felt, was being devalued.

In the first hours of freedom on 9 November it was already coming home to East Germans that their money meant nothing in the West, that their currency was worthless paper in the world outside the Wall. Regine knew that still further devaluations were in store for the freed citizenry storming through the checkpoints, that their voices, words, selves would all be marked down in the long, resounding bargain basement of the coming year.

IN A FOG OF PLENTY

Helmut is a pediatrician and a specialist in childhood sexuality. He and his second wife Marina were both born in 1956. They were children when the Wall was built. Its fall made them feel as though the ground were failing under their feet. Their sense of territoriality, of knowing where they were, vanished in a bubble-bright gleam of shop windows and TV lights.

"I only realized after I was there," Marina said, "what the economic and social system [in the West] meant. I'd only romanticized before. And when I came back, I was sick for a week. I lay in bed, suffering from West-shock. The shock consisted of realizing the *normality* of life there, that all the wealth and glitter was part of normal life. Breaking this taboo by crossing into no-man's-land was something fatal for me. You don't cross taboos so easily. I lost eight pounds after I came back."

In the weeks after the opening, both Helmut and Marina thought hard about the opportunities that had passed them by in their years of containment, about desires impossible to fulfill, and about the adjustments their altered state would require.

"With the opening of the Wall," Helmut explained, "three things changed in our daily lives. First, there was the phenomenon of the *Begrüssungsgeld*, greeting money, which we get from the Federal Republic. Just stop in the bank and pick it up, free! You're all automatically citizens of rich and generous West Germany. Can you imagine what that does to people's minds? To collect money in one day that equals a whole year's salary after exchange?

"Then there was the 'window effect' [the glazed, stunned impotence felt by first-time shoppers staring into Western store displays]. A true consumer shock. All these things one can buy in the West, the Mercedes and Audis and leather coats and stereos. The finest of everything on display in every corner store."

The discovery of wealth across the Wall prompted new, greedy, invidious examinations of the inequities of life at home.

"Third, there was the discovery of the privileges here, where the Central Committee of the Communist party lived in luxury, in Wandlitz [a walled-in compound that looked outwardly like a lower-middle-class suburb, but inwardly was stocked with expensive imports] and the trade union, how it had ripped the workers off."

Discourse became impoverished in the weeks following the opening. The only subject of discussion became the goods people lacked. "You couldn't talk with people about socialism anymore. Nor democracy! Well, we lack a democratic tradition here. For years the citizens have been deeply suspicious of politics, and Krenz, hell, nobody liked him. After visiting the West, people returned feeling they'd been duped. Even though many here enjoyed a higher standard of living than they would have in West Berlin, they didn't believe it anymore. With the opening of the Wall it was like the regime was saying, 'Go on over there, you idiot.' And the people answered, 'But we believed you before. And you yourself didn't believe the lies you have been telling us. Then kiss my ass. I give up. Germany, united Fatherland!' "

"That's where the greeting money comes in," added Marina. "It plays such an important role in people's fantasies. Our Jonah came up to us right after the Wall opened and said, 'All the other children already went to the West. Why can't we go?'

"I said to him, 'Because we don't have any West German marks.'

" 'That's okay,' he replied. 'There's *Begrüssungsgeld* in the West.'

"A married couple with children can each pick up a thousand deutschmarks, if they go to the [West German] bank separately. Then if they use two separate identity cards, they can even double that amount. If they only do it once, they can exchange that for 20,000 Eastmarks, which is more money in one day than they can earn in a year. That's tremendously unsettling.

"So we took Jonah with us to West Berlin. He kept saying, 'Where do we get our greeting money?' And I kept saying, 'Jonah, don't whine in public.'

"The U-Bahn was so full, you could hardly breathe, so we finally got out and walked instead. Then Jonah noticed, 'There are only big Western cars here. It smells better.' "

Helmut interrupted: "We finally had to put the brakes on him." And he began to reminisce oddly, a little hypnotically, about his own feeling of being in *Niemandsland,* a strange country neither here nor there, where the marks of the barbarous past still persist but are stripped of meaning and authority.

"Marina and I already knew what the Wall looked like when open, but still, you get this idiotic feeling that you're going through a barricade where people used to be shot at. It's very eerie. When I was a child, I used to fantasize about how I would escape. The white line on the street was always the crucial symbol. If I crossed that, I'd made it. Crossing that symbol, especially with Jonah there, was a very tense thing for me."

Helmut's days and nights are now fogged by a feeling like what Freud famously called the *unheimlich,* the unhomely, the uncanny. He feels suspended between two states, two homes, two ideologies, two identities. It is not a sensation recognizably akin to one of freedom.

"The Wall still exists," he remarks, "only not for us. The Vietnamese who work here are still confined to this territory. A week ago about twenty of them stood waiting for a line at the border opening, and as soon as the guards were busy, they rushed the crossing. I saw one interviewed on West Berlin television. He's now asking for asylum there. I don't think he could speak much German. He kept repeating, 'Shitty socialism. Shitty socialism.'

"Communism is not and cannot be a science as it has claimed. It's a religion like all the others. And the attempt to introduce socialism was always tied to Stalin. You can't force the masses to be happy according to your own rules."

In a mist of uncertainty, in the mixed-up time after the great Historic Moment, Helmut and Marina look for new rules, their own rules, for happiness.

INSTANT KINSHIP AS A SYMBOL FALLS

"We were speechless," so many of them say, the East Germans; they say it over and over, describing their reactions to the first glimpse of the West, making speech of their own silencing. "We were speechless," they say. It was all "*Wahnsinn!*"—"insane!"

Frau Gruner remembers another moment of speechlessness, the *Stunde Null*, the moment when the war ended and the guns fell silent. This liminal moment in modern German history furnishes an analogy for the events of 9 November. The opening of the Wall was the *Stunde Null* the first postwar generation of Germans, of Helmut and

Marina, Beate, Hildegard, and Bert. For these men and women, old enough to remember the special and life-altering meaning of the Wall, young enough to imagine a life without it, it was the hour the battles ended and the standard discourses died, the hour of great and stunning change, the central moment of their lives.

At that hour the categories of everyday existence, old categories of East and West, communist and capitalist, friend and foe, lost their meaning. People couldn't believe it would last. They walked around smiling, as if they were pulling a dirty trick on someone.

The opening of the Wall was "saturated with emotional quality," in the words of the anthropologist Benjamin Sapir,[1] because the Wall itself was steeped in symbolism. In it, the whole system of oppositions that constituted the Cold War was summed up and condensed. It was a symbol that both structured and encapsulated a variety of local, national, and international relations. The Wall embodied many meanings in exceedingly simple form. Tearing it down, more than any other particular event in Eastern Europe in 1989, accelerated the pace and affirmed the inevitability of the collapse of the Cold War.

As the structures and categories of everyday life broke down, an inchoate and all-embracing sense of national "communitas" swept in to take their place.[2] During this first week in a joined Berlin, all social relations were simplified as conventional categories of behavior were ignored. Ordered ordinary life surrendered its intricacy and complexity. In place of the fine discriminations and hierarchies that generally governed action in the quotidian world of sidewalk, office, and home, a variety of broad, mythic constructs—brotherhood, Germanness, freedom—intervened to unify disparate norms and build a sense of unanimity among the diverse, intermingling groups. All Germans in East and West Berlin, who before the opening had coexisted in complex, tense, and carefully mediated relations, were suddenly loving brothers in every appearance of pure immediacy and utter spontaneity, a chemistry the Germans call *Verbrüderung*.

The spontaneity was, of course, superficial. If anything, the mystic oneness of the jaded West Germans and the goggle-eyed first-time *flaneurs* from the East was more thoroughly mediated than their usual interactions. On the one hand, there was an exaggerated appeal to the mediating influence of myth, to the concept of *Gesamtdeutschland* or the "entire Germany." On the other hand, there was an elaboration of banal rituals to serve as material support for the mythic concepts. Drinking, buying, visiting, the repeated rites that accompanied a general increase in sociability, served to imprint the grand new unity unconsciously on their practitioners, in a sort of practice drill of universal love.

The experience of the opening, the *Verbrüderung*, created a sense of German community that will last much longer than the event itself. Most important, it mediated, organized, and structured that emerging community in ways that were specific, solid, and lasting. In particular, the first reactions of the East Germans—their intimidation and passivity, their stunned shock and their occasional sheer terror at the wealth of the West—created a pattern for future interactions. This pattern persists, however deeply drowned under the voices of loudspeakers preaching oneness and the television newsmen talking about freedom.

AND THEN—ENNUI

Perhaps, in this somber light, the most sensible reaction to the opening of the Wall was that of Arnim, a handsome fifty-year-old East Berliner whom many would call a ne'er-do-well. He slept through it. Not until next morning when he showed up at work did he discover what had happened the night before: the banners flying, the klieg lights illuminating the serpentine graffiti, the rush of feet exploring the great unknown boulevards, the strange side streets, the vistas of the glorious future, the dead ends.

Not till another two days had passed, till the weekend, did he go to West Berlin. "I had to work!" he excused himself, referring to his new job as a ticket taker in a cinema, which he had gotten two weeks before. "It opened on a Thursday, and I couldn't find time to go over till Saturday."

In the three years since I had known Arnim, this was his first regular job. One fall day in 1986 he decided to stay home from work. For the next three years he survived by eating very little, drinking quite a lot, and bartering away antiques he inherited from his parents.

When he finally made it to West Berlin, it was almost by accident. "It was like this," he explained. "On Saturday morning, I crossed over, into a neighborhood in Wedding. And hell, I didn't know where I was! It'd been twenty-eight years since I'd been in the West, and back then I was just a kid. Didn't go over there much anyway before the Wall went up. What for? I wandered around the streets and looked at all the clean facades on the apartment buildings. I ran into a woman puttering around in her yard, and asked her where I was and how to get to KuDamm. She looked at me and said, 'You're from the East, aren't you?' I said, 'Yes, I am.' And she gave me ten deutschmarks!"

Weeks later he was still baffled by the unfamiliar paper. "I've never had deutschmarks before," he says. "Those were my very first. We don't know what to do with this money. I still haven't spent it! Everything is so expensive in the West, I can't go out drinking or do anything. I came back after looking around. That was enough for the first time."

He doesn't seem impressed by the strange mirror-city that had always been left off East German maps. It confuses him. "On Sunday when I went over again, I brought along two bottles of beer, and I thought I'd give one to the border guard on our side and one to the guard in the West. A nice kind of gesture. But then there was such a crowd at the border that I ended up keeping them and drank them myself."

4

Becoming Socialist

After the uprising of the 17th June
The Secretary of the Writer's Union
Had leaflets distributed on the Stalinallee
Stating that the people
Had forfeited the confidence of the government. . . .
          Would it not be easier
In that case for the government
To dissolve the people
And elect another?

—Bertolt Brecht, The Solution

DONNING THE SOCIALIST CLOAK

The fact that East Berliners experienced the opening of
the Wall in such different ways is a point worth stressing if

only because the ubiquitous TV cameras of the world broadcast the event to the West as a monolithic, mass, unquestioning celebration. The variety of individual reactions to the collapse of the East German system was actually almost endless and was conditioned by the variety of lives led under that system. Life with the Wall, life under socialism, had not been all of one hue.

This simple fact contradicts a central tenet of the way the West sees the East. The theory of "totalitarianism"—of complete state regimentation of everyday life—put forward by observers from capitalist countries as a comprehensive description of their communist counterparts, is inadequate to account for the complexity of experience in those states.[1] It may accurately describe the goals of the regimes ruling Soviet bloc countries, but it falls short of depicting the effects of their policies. It omits the intricate strategies of resistance and evasion, complicity and secrecy, that characterized (in uneasy combinations and alternations) the everyday life of the people.

At least in East Germany, totalitarianism never existed, but it served the interests of the ruling elite within the GDR, as much as those of Western observers, to propound theories of total control. What better mechanism of control than to convince the people that, from cradle to grave, Big Brother's electric eye was upon them? In fact, Big Brother, in the form of the Stasi, *was* nearly everywhere. The Stasi kept files on one-third of all residents, but ever-expanding records in mushrooming file cabinets could not keep pace with the ever-multiplying resistance, passive and active, in daily practice. Big Brother was often blinkered and confused, bluffed and deceived.

The state could not effectively police all expression and movement. Nor did its strictures mean the same thing to all citizens. To confuse the theory of totalitarianism with the practice of everyday life is to mistake an ideal type for an empirical reality, a fundamental confusion of the scientific model with the phenomenon it seeks to describe. The question we might ask of East Berliners is what control and its opposites, freedom and choice, meant to them in the context of their immediate experience.

Even among the most loyal and submissive citizens, many continually practiced a form of what Claude Lévi-Strauss called *bricolage,*[2] reshuffling and relabeling the ideological residue they received from the state. In this way, no less than citizens of capitalist states, they attempted to establish a sphere of private intentionality. This chapter examines how two "good" East Germans, blue-ribbon products of the socialist state, arrived at their socialist identities and the different meanings and capabilities of their acquired selfhood as citizen/subjects of the GDR.

SUSTAINED BY NOSTALGIA

Regine is a fifty-three-year-old documentary filmmaker in East Berlin. She lives in a four-story apartment complex built for workers in the 1920s, in a functionally conceived, two-room flat with a balcony overlooking a courtyard checkerboarded with private gardens. It is the buying and selling of such garden plots, with perhaps new walls to make them exclusive, that she now sees spreading like a plague over the East German landscape, as it is colonized and parceled out by the capitalist West.

"We're afraid," she says, "of being swallowed—I mean in a really primitive way—by West Germany. That Kohl!

I'd punch him in his snout if I had the chance. He thinks that because he has more money he's superior and can do with us what he wants.

"You know, you fight your whole life for some principle—I say this while fully acknowledging all the horrible things done under the name socialism—and now, when it finally seems as if you have a chance of setting forth this principle, of finally beginning, they all want to throw it away. The economic situation is also not good, and getting worse. It's understandable what the people want, but very sad. Right now we're really at wit's end."

Regine speaks of herself almost as a socialist Lone Ranger. For her, addressing the collective good takes on the moral authority of an intensely personal cause. She sees herself as an individualist, a defender of principle. She is arguably the most socialist person I know. She even describes herself that way. "I guess I'm socialist by nature," she affirms.

She works at the German Film Association (DEFA), the state documentary film studio. Her great goal in life, she recalls, was to make films in support of Third World liberation movements. From early on she cultivated friendships with people from developing countries, and studied film technique, but her political enthusiasm got in the way of her career. She wanted to make movies about real people, not the "caricatures" the regime wanted to see represented. To this day Regine has not been able to fulfill her goal. After completing three documentaries on other topics, she was denied further opportunities to put her ideas on film.

Yet her pulse beats to the rhythm of the *Internationale*. Socialism is in her blood. She is the direct heir of a strong progressive political tradition, her family's story encapsulating much of the history of the twentieth-century German left. In the 1920s and 1930s, her grandfather was the leader of the Social Democratic party (SPD) in a small rural district near Leipzig. He kept the party's books and maintained their membership lists. In the declining years of the Weimar Republic, the Social Democratic party and the Communist party (KPD) refused to form a united front against the Nazis, thus enabling the ultimate Nazi triumph. In 1933, Hitler declared both parties illegal. When, in 1934, the local Nazis asked Regine's grandfather to turn over the SPD records, he refused and became subject to constant harassment under the Third Reich.

In April 1946, the revived German Communist party, its leadership newly returned from a 12-year Moscow exile, forced a union in East Germany with the also renascent, and larger and wealthier, Social Democrat party. This combined party was named the Socialist Unity party (SED). Regine's grandfather rejected the dissolution of his party and refused to join the new SED. When the local SED asked him to turn over the membership records of the Social Democrats, he again refused.

"I didn't betray the lists to the Nazis," he said. "I won't with the SED either."

Today, in 1990, with a newly reformed SPD in the East, the issue of the party's compulsory union with the SED in 1946 is again coming to the fore. Many of the recent resettlers to the West are asking for automatic membership in the West German SPD, claiming they were forced to join the Communists after the war, but had never given up their sympathy for the SPD. Some residents of the GDR have also applied for membership in the West German SPD, rather than participating in the reorganization of their own party.

The reorganized East German SPD, meanwhile, has derived a transient and paradoxical cachet from having been swallowed by the Communists 40 years earlier. Since its name was for so long missing from East German ballots, it has an aura of newness and cleanness. Unlike the satellite parties co-opted and corrupted into collaboration with the regime, the SPD (one of the most venerable left-wing parties in Europe) looks fresh and untainted to many bewildered voters.

During the Third Reich, Regine's father was discriminated against in both education and employment because of his father's reputation as a Social Democrat and anti-Fascist. Hence he grew up without obtaining an apprenticeship to learn a trade, as did his peers from more politically compliant families. Although Regine's grandfather refused to join the new Socialist Unity party, her father, who hadn't shared the same antagonisms against the Communists during Weimar, and who perhaps saw a way of recovering some respectability, jumped at the invitation to join the SED.

Until the building of the Wall in 1961, young workers in the GDR were in short supply. Many were leaving for West Germany, where wages were higher and the Marshall Plan was stimulating economic expansion. Thus untrained workers such as Regine's father had exceptional opportunities in East Germany to rise to leadership positions. GDR industrial policy encouraged young, motivated workers with raw ability to take an active part in reconstruction. In these unusual circumstances Regine's father became the foreman of his shift at the local power station, and a valued worker in the postwar state. By his own account, he also learned a great deal from the few older experts trained during Weimar who were still available to provide the expertise and continuity necessary for economic expansion in GDR industry in the 1950s and 1960s. The late 1960s however, saw radical changes.

"My father said," Regine remembers, "that back in the 1950s all social groups would go to the *Kneipe*, the neighborhood bar. Teachers, normal workers, our bourgeoisie, everyone could be found in the same *Kneipe*. That has never before existed in other capitalist countries, not in the Federal Republic, not in France. We overcame the most critical class distinctions back then, in the beginning. We produced art for the people. In what was called the *Bitterfeld* movement, writers went into the factories. That was progress, something very positive in history."

For Regine, in her twenties at the time, these were the great days of the GDR, a time of limitless opportunity for all ages and backgrounds, a time of sacrifices made worthwhile by a genuine common spirit.

"Between the ages of 50 and 54, my father returned to school to get more technical training. Imagine that! A man of that age going back to evening school, not for status or self-gain, but because the knowledge was needed where he worked."

Later, "everything was deformed. It became rigid, fossilized. This all changed slowly, so that by the 1970s, only political criteria were important in promotional policy and industrial planning.

"My father was never one of those who didn't speak his mind. When he thought something was wrong, he always spoke freely to his coworkers and to the bureaucrats above him. He was also critical of the Party, especially of the immense paperwork coming from above." And, Regine claims, he carried through on his goals. "Workers in industries were more critical of the authorities than we intellectuals were. They were needed; the state couldn't do without them. But in the last ten to fifteen years, everything has stagnated, and become senseless. It has rotted away the substance of the people. The structure of the SED apparatus became more refined in the last ten years. They brought everything under their control.

"You get a sense of that by looking at the train system—it's never punctual anymore." The once-active citizenry has been reduced to passivity. "Everything is set by the Party from above, and below, on the production end, the people just follow."

Regine's critique of why things went wrong follows that of many other GDR intellectuals. In each of their accounts there was a fall from grace, from a now-lost valorized moment when classes labored happily together and democracy seemed on the verge of realization. Such intellectuals often seem to have a brightly colored Socialist Realist mural in the backs of their minds, showing smiling workers and smiling bureaucrats clasping hands, a mural now defaced by the adolescent whims of History. In each account, the party slowly took control of all facets of administration, with no other public organs and no democratic controls from below to counteract its monopoly on power. The state began to resemble an authoritarian command system, with far-reaching consequences for the centralized system of economic planning.

Plan fulfillment was pursued with religious fervor. It took priority over all other considerations of public policy, such as environmental protection or investment and marketing strategies. With no reinvestment policy, the country essentially lived off its capital for 40 years, until it was nearly depleted. Socialism degenerated into a type of administrative centralism, in which groups of civil servants—party apparatchiks—unquestioningly carried through the orders of the Central Committee of the Politburo, a small group of aging men.

Each of the recently socialist countries, from Rumania to Russia, is rife with accounts of the sclerotic excesses of the inner circles, doddering, despotic, increasingly divorced from their popular base, and ever more insecure about their own legitimacy as rulers. The Western consumer luxuries of Wandlitz, the leaders' private compound, were a nine days wonder in East Germany once the press was free to report them.

The public learned, for example, that Honecker used to order a roadblock preventing public access to the Autobahn when he traveled in his Swedish Volvo from Berlin to his hunting lodge. They learned that servants at the lodge fattened the deer and drove them within Honecker's shooting range. Even in sport the leaders had no sense of fair play.

Regine asserts that "the corruption doesn't bother me. I know others get disturbed by it all, but I've never concerned myself much with material things. You know, I don't need that much to be satisfied." And she repeats: "By my very nature I'm socialist, I guess."

Regine, like many other intellectuals, defines her socialism in nostalgia. She looks back, with a romantic's eye, on a democratic and productive state now faded into the past. It has very little to do with her own experience, but seems summed up in the figure of her idealized father.

"My father was a class-conscious thinker," she says, "but not a Marxist. He had such an open mind. He spoke with men from the church, although he himself was an atheist with perhaps religious moments. He took in children from problem families and raised them with us so that they would obtain some self-respect in the schools, being associated with a local respectable family. He taught mathematics and physics after school when they couldn't find anyone else.

"For me, socialism had nothing to do with Honecker. For me, it was about humans, about underprivileged humans, and we are to use our time on this earth to fight for them. After all, what do we really know from Marx, such a complicated thinker?

"The worse thing about our leadership here, what I hold most against them, is how they oppressed people's productivity. That is precisely the opposite of socialism, which was supposed to free humans, to emancipate them. That is at the heart of their crimes, not the corruption."

In one of his conversations with Bertolt Brecht in the 1930s, Walter Benjamin said of theorists such as the much-loathed Hungarian Georg Lukacs, that "With these people . . . you just cannot build a state." Brecht replied, "Or only a state, but not a community. They are quite simply enemies of production. Production makes them uneasy. It can't be trusted. It is the unpredictable. You never know where it will end. And they themselves do not want to produce. They want to play the apparatchik and supervise others."[3]

Regine echoes Brecht's criticism with uncanny precision some 50 years later. She excoriates the party leadership for a fundamental lack of imagination. Obsessed with their plans, they failed to embrace the spontaneous, the uncontrolled, that is, human labor as Marx delineated it, producing a life-world from chaotic raw materials.

In this aspect, as *genuine, fulfilling* production, labor always has something of the unexpectable and uncontrollable about it, a genuine leap into the unknown and free future. Under the GDR leadership, labor became merely the fulfillment of preset standards. The "Plan" had nothing to do with the Marxian emancipation of human capabilities, but instead was a horizon of effort dictated by the state's techniques of social control. The result was a monolithic state, but a nonexistent community. The state merely presided over a multiplicity of thwarted individual hopes, stifled and intensely private expectations.[4]

The private conception of socialism that Regine developed in response to these conditions took shape as a compensation for their constraints. The state's perceived lack of faith in spontaneity cut off Regine's capacity to believe in a free future, so she romanticized a freedom located in her family and in a past imperceptibly gilded by her imagination. The state's perceived mistrust of genuine production, its fixation on control, caused her to turn to a private form of production to vindicate her existence. Regine became a producer of discourse. The moments she finds most valuable are bound up with the work of *telling*, of expressing herself and helping others to express themselves. Work offered little meaning or fulfillment for Regine under the conditions the state offered, but she is a worker and an artificer of her individual life-world, through her words and stories.

"My family," she says, "always served as a model for me about what socialism could be like. I was much closer to my father than to my mother. We never merely had political discussions, but we also did things. We cared for animals—we lived on a farm—and cared for our neighbors. We were never schooled politically, but learned politics instinctively, as the workers do."

Regine speaks rather patronizingly of her mother, who "came out of a *Beamte*, civil servant, family; my father out of a lower class, the working class. Perhaps that explains their different capabilities." Her mother was kind and generous, but insecure about her intermediate position in society and intent on preserving her tenuous class position. Her father, on the other hand, knew who he was and could act on it. His identity was a productive one. His only asset, as a proletarian, was his labor. He made no pretense to having any other, which explains to Regine his great capacity for personal development. His only field for improvement was himself, his body, mind, and material condition, and that meant a willingness and even eagerness to change.

It is this unschooled instinctive skill that she prizes most about her father. He *did*, he *produced*, rather than *argued* or *said*.

"My father always had access to the intellectual milieu, and he knew many intellectuals, but he always presented himself as a worker, which, in fact, he was. My family gave me so much in my life that I never could forget them. I visited them regularly, at least once a month after I moved to Berlin."

When I first met Regine she confided in me that her father had lost interest in life and was beginning to drink. Such an intelligent, loving man, she said. She couldn't understand how he could do this. Ever more frequently she argued with him, until finally she took him in her arms and shook him violently, threatening not to see him anymore if he continued drinking. Her love for him was too great to see him willfully waste away. She promised to visit him weekly only if he would agree to quit drinking.

I had told Regine about my interest in autobiographies, in people's life stories and their relation to political history. Regine was stimulated to undertake a joint project with her father. She began to record his life story. Each week he eagerly awaited her visit, having spent the week before preparing. He recalled important incidents in his life, centering on different political events and how the workers in his factory reacted to them. Each week she wrote up what he had told her and the following week read it with him during her visit. He would break in and make corrections. "No, it wasn't quite like that," he would say or would add other incidents which, after a week of reflection, seemed equally significant. Regine observed that their weekly meetings gave him a new sense of life, a *Lebenssinn*; instead of turning to the bottle to forget, he used Regine's project as an incentive to remember.

He and Regine thus constructed a private history of the regime under which, the times through which, they'd lived. The work gave Regine the same satisfaction that her documentaries had. She was constructing a self and an ideological stance for that self.

Her father's story subtly subverted her version of him as a tireless producer. His reminiscences turned gradually into a long examination of how an entire generation was perverted into passivity. The workers in East Germany never actually took power in the industries for the simple reason that they never trusted their own ability to rule. They had had no experience with power, either during Weimar or the Third Reich. That was why the party had such an easy time establishing control. Its members were convinced of their legitimacy, of their right to command, and the workers, lacking training in democracy, deferred to party leaders in all crucial decisions. Nor did the new state encourage them to think for themselves. By the early 1950s, debate in party meetings was discouraged. Assemblies became dull affairs where members were expected to agree unanimously to whatever programs were proposed. The party was their guardian and ruled in their interests: They were to follow its commands.

The authoritative instructions of the state replaced initiative; listening, for the citizenry, took the place of doing. For Regine personally, the only sphere for initiative lay in weaving a fragile counter-discourse to the weighty words of the party, turning her father's words into a private speaking-against, a contra-diction, a local and tenuous act of reflection, an alternative voicing of possibilities and hopes. She became the thwarted speaker rather than the fulfilled doer and so (though she would not have said this) had her father. Still she groped to find a vision of socialism that could endure, for an idyll of fulfilling labor to which she could cling and give voice.

"My father loved my mother tremendously. He respected and honored her throughout his life. Three days before his death, I was sitting by his bedside. He had been dying for nearly a year, and his body had shrunk to nothing. Often when I sat there I wept uncontrollably—but not out of sadness. I told him, 'Papa, I am crying for joy, joy that I have been able to live through so much with you all these years, that I have learned and shared so much with you that has been invaluable to me. Our friendship has so enriched my life, I am so grateful.'

"I had always shared more with him than with my mother, and he knew that. He then said to me, 'Your mother doesn't have the same intellectual capacity as we do, but we shouldn't ever neglect her for that.'

"I was deeply moved. It seemed such a profound philosophy! For me that was socialism."

There is an element of quiet sentimentalism in Regine's "profound philosophy," a touch of the self-congratulatory condescension intellectuals feel in indulging the less gifted. Yet it is moving in its own right as an attempt to salvage meaning from the contradictions of her own experience. Redefining socialism in these terms allows Regine to maintain an identity outwardly acceptable to, yet inwardly separate from, the state's discourse. She tells herself to herself and makes herself whole.

ASK AND IT SHALL (NOT) BE GIVEN

Hildegard, now aged forty, has never been able to determine exactly why she and her husband Bert remained in the GDR. Neither was a particularly committed socialist; neither felt an ideological compulsion comparable to Regine's. Nor did they enjoy any special privileges, either from inheritance or their own capabilities. They did not have especially fulfilling work and they possessed neither a country house nor a big, beautiful apartment.

In many ways, they were moderately comfortable *Kleinbürger*, an East German version of the American lower middle class. The term (and its opposite, *Grossbürger*) refers less to the size of one's pocketbook than to levels of taste and status. The *Grossbürger* has *Bildung* (education and manners) and a sense of security about his position. He incarnates the stolidity and self-possession of burgherdom. The *Kleinbürger*,[5] by contrast, is a sort of fallen bourgeois, or perhaps a thinly bourgeoisified proletarian. Trapped on the lower margins of middle-class existence, maintaining a veneer of respectability, he struggles to keep his balance, swaying over abysses of humiliation, perpetually at risk of being exposed as *declassé*.

In this tenuous social position, however, Hildegard and

her husband fulfilled the ideal model the state propounded for its people. The GDR encouraged its citizens to be *Kleinbürger*, not strictly classless but a mix-and-match of desirable class characteristics. The *Kleinbürger* combined a proletarian origin and income level appropriate to the citizenry of a self-styled worker's and farmer's state with something of the conservatism and safeness of the middle-class householder. His anxiety about status made him resistant to radical change and thus an agreeably compliant subject of an increasingly bureaucratized state apparatus.

Hildegard knew very well that she fit this description closely. As a happily married woman with two children, a regular job, and regular husband in a regular apartment, she was a picture-book version of what the GDR wanted its citizens to be. And since she had no relatives in West Germany, she was made of the ideal stuff, the untainted *prima materia*, from which the state constructed its most loyal adherents.

To encourage bonds between itself and its citizens, the GDR established dependencies. The state tried to represent each casual happening of everyday life as a co-project, a cooperative effort, between itself and the individual. In reward for the citizen's conformity to the ideal of *Kleinbürgertum*, the state protected him from the extremes of poverty (the GDR never had homeless or hungry people) and injustice. This cradle-to-grave strategy did increase dependency, much as the state wanted; but it also increased the citizens' resentment. For as expectations rose and self-initiatives declined, the state couldn't keep pace in fulfilling its citizens' needs. The people adopted the passive stance the state wanted, but they became yawning pits of unsatisfied demand.

Hildegard's expectations were never that great, she felt,

but they were always several steps ahead of the ability of the state to meet them. In the early 1980s, they began to take written form. Much as Regine had turned to forms of self-expression to vent her dissatisfaction, Hildegard began her career of protest as a teller of tales with a remarkable series of *Eingaben* or legal petitions. Unlike Regine in her private narratives, Hildegard took her frustration out in highly public, official forms of address.

The *Eingabe* is a form of direct appeal, either oral or written, whereby a citizen can appeal to the responsible authorities for a remedy of a problem. A 1975 law required authorities to respond within four weeks. The petitions allowed the citizenry a licit means of responding to and interrogating the economic and political power structure, a legal privilege rare enough in capitalist countries. They only intermittently produced results, of course. Their primary function, perhaps, was as a forum for mutual expression. The authorities were forced to defend themselves and the citizens were encouraged to articulate their needs in a mode the state could comprehend. They translated desire into official form.

Hildegard wrote numerous petitions over the years, on subjects ranging from the sublime to the ridiculous, from cabbages to kings. In them, she expressed her sense of socialism not as thwarted production, but as unmet needs. Unlike Regine, she retained her faith in the future, her hope for ultimate satisfaction, but it came at the expense of her independence, her sense of private identity. More and more, her petitions express and consummate a bargain. She presented herself more and more as what the state wanted her to be, in order to get from it what she wanted.

Eingaben have a long tradition in Germany, from the time of Frederick the Second, when citizens wrote regularly begging his aid in fixing roads or settling disputes, to the Third Reich, when even prisoners in concentration camps wrote local authorities asking for better rations or longer exercise periods. In both Germanies the tradition continued after the war, but it became more important in East Germany than in the West. In East Germany there was no institutionalized political authority to secure citizen protection from bureaucratic authorities.

In 1953, a petition by construction workers on Stalinallee in East Berlin, sent to Prime Minister Otto Grotewohl, started a state-wide worker uprising. Laws strengthening the right to use *Eingaben* were passed in 1961, 1966, 1969, and 1975. By the mid-1980s, all companies were employing extra help to answer the petitions as the law required them to do. Political authorities began to monitor *Eingaben* as a way of measuring citizen discontent. A large proportion of petitions in the early 1980s concerned the difficulty of finding apartments, but by the mid-1980s growing numbers of people were complaining about the state's restrictions on travel.

Hildegard's petitions followed a pattern similar to that of her fellow citizens. She wrote her first *Eingabe* in 1981. She phrased her appeal with care, employing a formal, polite style. As her pleas met with success, they became more forceful and more frequent.

In May 1987, for example, she appealed to the People's Own Company (VEB) Shoe Fabric for tennis shoes for her two sons. The company made no verbal response to her letter. Rather, it offered what the responsible officials no doubt considered a still better reply: Within two weeks, two pairs of shoes in the right sizes arrived in the mail. Hildegard was almost disappointed to get the mute package of goods. She preferred *responses*, through which the somnolescent authorities governing her life assumed voices and entered into a dialogue. Letters, memoranda, gave her something to stand on, somehow more satisfying than the silent presence of a mere pair of shoes. Documents comprised a conversation with the state; the shoes were only footwear. In August 1987, she appealed to VEB Untertrikotagen "Antiseda" in Karl-Marx-Stadt for sport shirts for her sons. Herr Petzold of Antiseda wrote back, saying he was responsible for production, not distribution, but he sympathized with her "extreme situation," and would send her two shirts as soon as possible if she would send the sizes needed. Now there was something she could hold on to.

Emboldened, Hildegard wrote the same month to the Minister of Health about an upsetting sign she had seen in the hospital where her two sons were recovering from diarrhea acquired while vacationing in a state-owned spa. The sign read: "No information will be given out during visiting hours." Since that was the only time she could visit her children in the hospital, and since she had no telephone to call the doctors, she was outraged and pleaded for "new rules" and "more human" interaction by the medical staff. The Ministry assured her they had read her letter "with careful attention," and were going to discuss it further in terms of "each person's individual responsibility." She was asked to wait for another response. She never received it.

In October 1987, Hildegard wrote to VEB "Reh" complaining that for the last year and a half she had been unable to find any ski pants. She concluded somewhat dejectedly, "I still have a little hope that I'll happen onto someone with a soft heart who will listen." This time the heavens smiled. Her hopes were answered. Two weeks later the long-awaited ski pants arrived.

In 1988 she wrote two petitions. In the first she asked for replacement of a sofa pillow lost by the state-owned dry cleaners. She hardly expected a replacement, but was infuriated when she didn't even eke out a reply. In the second letter, she turned to the Minister for Consumer Goods. In this petition, for the first time, she rose above the personal to complain about the situation in the country generally. She asked the minister, "Where will it all lead?" The difficulty was trying to buy white summer shoes with closed toes. The shoe problem had reared its head again. She had been trying for two years and could find only colored shoes. When she finally found white shoes they all had open toes. She decided to go ahead and buy them anyway, for 175 marks (20 percent of a month's salary), but there were none in her size. She thought of buying them anyway, hoping to exchange with another woman who might also have bought the wrong size. Instead she decided to write the letter. Such situations could not go on.

The minister sent her letter on to the VEB Kombinat Shoes Weissenfels. The director responded in July. He sent no shoes, but plenty of information. The manufacture of shoes had gone up 6.5 percent in the last year, the state subsidizing production in a planned and correct manner. Furthermore, the company would distribute a wide selection of middle-priced women's shoes in the second half of the year. Hildegard should wait and have confidence in the wisdom of planning.

In February 1989, Hildegard (still wearing colored shoes with open toes) went to the store and bought a box of peppermint tea bags that produced "the bitterest tea" she had ever drunk, "thoroughly undrinkable or perhaps fit for some medicinal purpose." A petition immediately resulted. The VEB Pharmaceutical Work of Halle wrote back that they had tested the content of the tea bags both for quantity and quality, and found nothing abnormal. They hoped that despite this unpleasant experience, she "would remain our customer in the future." In August 1989 she wrote the bishop of a Catholic diocese complaining that his criticism of a local priest was unjustified. The bishop too responded with a long, defensive letter.

These successes in eliciting discourse, if not results, from the powerful gave Hildegard courage for her greatest and most comprehensive effort. She was saving her *saeva indignatio* for a petition to the president of the Parliament, Horst Sindermann. Written on 8 September 1989, two months before the opening of the border, it concerned her application to accompany her husband on a trip to West Germany. Bert had been granted permission to visit his aunt in the West for her 65th birthday. Hildegard, however, had been denied permission.

She explained herself to Sindermann in detail: thirty-nine years old, educated as a secondary school teacher, an occupation she had practiced for four years. Later she had two sons, to whom she devoted herself as mother, at the same time working in a company where she had just been awarded an "Activist Medal." Her sons consistently received certificates "For Good Learning in Socialist Schools." But her "pride over this achievement" was of limited satisfaction. The certificates were "no security for an entire life." Instead, she offers her whole life up as a self-evident socialist achievement, a lien on that deserved security. She had now been married for 19 years, in a marriage "neither worse nor better than others." She and her husband sought "to remain interested in life, to have definite hobbies, to cultivate family tradition, and to maintain a large circle of friends."

For page after page Hildegard paints herself as the ideal GDR woman, her family as the almost apocalytically perfect fulfillment of the Family Law Book of 1965. Hers was a marriage of mutual love and respect. The children were an essential part of her happiness, raised to be respectable, responsible citizens.

That was only one side of their experience, however. She just as thoroughly describes the other. Her husband has few relatives left in the GDR. Driven from East Prussia in 1946, most of his family sought refuge in West Germany. Why should she be punished for her in-laws' mistake? She, after all, had no relatives of her own who deserted to the West. It was important for her to maintain contact with her husband's aunt, who had faithfully maintained contact with them all these years.

She quotes the 1988 law allowing wives and husbands to travel together. She explains how she went to the authorities to appeal, how she had to wait in long lines, and how they rejected her claims. Rejection for her meant the rejection of her accomplishments as a citizen. "I stood outside with the certainty that I am here, here to stay—forever in perpetuity."

She emphasizes her loyalty: "I was born here and I cannot and do not want to leave my *Heimat*." She had no thoughts about leaving—"legally or illegally"—that was out of the question. Proudly she flaunts her taut resistance to the sirens of the West, as against her fellow citizens' susceptibility to blandishments. "Are they all so strong?" she sneers of the deserters.

Her family already knows Poland and Czechoslovakia and Hungary well. They need—need! need!—to vacation elsewhere. She asks, "Is there a development [pending], or is this the last word?"

She ends her letter in tones that might be thought ironic, but which ring, when read in context, with a pathetic, almost agonizing earnestness. "Have trust in us and build on the decades of our good upbringing!" She pleads with her state—the workers' state, her state—to trust her. She had cited to the authorities their own order of things and herself as the model of a state-produced personality, *Kleinbürger* to the core. Now she entreats the GDR: Have faith in me! Reward me! I am what I am, who you think I am, unquestioningly your servant, your creation. If only they would recognize her for what she was, ski pants would abound, white shoes in all styles would rain like manna from the heavens, and visa stamps would spring up like mushrooms on her passport.

LAMBS TO THE SLAUGHTER

The petition reveals the ultimate pathos of Hildegard's stance. Her reams of *Eingaben* seem a form of self-assertion against the state, but they are only a personification of lack, of yearning. The self she asserts exists only as a vacuum of want, a shell, an emptiness molded in the state's image, to tempt the authorities into filling it with the desired goods— shoes, ski pants, vacations. Hildegard actually effaces herself in an ecstasy of need.

Regine's intensely private fantasies of fulfillment allowed her to preserve a fetishized but still personally satisfying version of the public sphere, of democracy, of productive action. By contrast, Hildegard articulated herself in the *actual* public sphere of the GDR, which encouraged only passivity, dependency, and incessant demand.

The life-world of capitalism preserves a public ideology

of production, community, and democratic choice. In the private sphere the reality of comprehensive social control makes itself evident: the living room with its dominating TV, the kitchen crammed with canned goods and frozen dinners, the bedroom where love is made according to the advertisements—all are strategic points corrupted by the values of a consumer society. In the public sphere the individual has the illusion of freedom. In private life he or she is reduced to a passive buyer, to dependency and need.

Socialism as practiced in the Eastern bloc reversed the model. Retreating to the private sphere, Regine was free to retain control over her identity, not just personally but politically, free even to redefine "socialism" to her own satisfaction. Her rooms, her everyday experiences, remained uncolonized. Telling stories to herself between four walls, she created a space of resistance and independent social consciousness few ordinary citizens in capitalist society could preserve.

The public realm, by contrast, was for East Germans the locus of pure, individualized, and isolating dependency. Citizens approached the state like abject Puritans entreating an angry God. The state encouraged its subjects to be consumers, not by insinuating itself into their living rooms, but by transforming their most public and overtly social acts into pleas and expressions of need. It was politics that was consumerized in the GDR.

Trained to think of their social selves as vacuums to be filled by a benevolent if erratic distributive apparatus; educated to give voice not to creative aspirations or ambitions to achieve but to their needs; used to seeing themselves, in public, as submissive mirrors of a Great Giver watching from on high, East Germans understandably reacted to the store windows of the KuDamm with a madcap shopping spree. Socialism unwittingly played into capitalism's hands in creating a virgin consuming class. The two systems meshed with paradoxical perfection. Far from encountering alien devotees of an utterly alien system, capitalism found in the stunned visitors an unexpected, ready, and all-too-welcome bounty, its very own *hypocrite lecteur, semblable, frère*. The GDR merely served up its passive populace on capitalism's altar. Socialism had trained them to desire. Capitalism stepped in to let them buy.

As for Hildegard's last petition, the East German state had long before given up any vestige of mutual trust. The Ministry for Internal Affairs responded curtly that her situation did not meet the "legal requirements" to travel in capitalist countries. Two months later, the regime, having lost its authority, opened its borders and made the question moot. In another month the Ministry for Internal Affairs was dissolved. Five months later, impressed by better buys abroad, the people voted, in effect, to eliminate the state itself.

5

Walled In Without a Home:
Exile of the Spirit
in the GDR State

All the time they were creating
What has destroyed them,
And they fall with the burden
They built.
—Friedrich Georg Junger, *Ultima Ratio*

A DIVIDED COUNTRY

Socialism and capitalism both sought to manage the basic populations under their control through one basic technique: the creation of needs. Capitalism generated these needs by furnishing a stunning satiation, an addictive array of goods and services. Socialism worked through a system of fear, deprivation, and punishment. The two approaches interlocked. The end result of each was dependency.

Looking back, one may wonder why the dependencies the socialist state erected proved so fragile, for convincing loyalties failed to emerge from the years of constructing a socialist citizenry. Not even Hildegard, who, through her petitions, effectively made herself into the image of GDR womanhood, remained faithful for long. Gainsaying all her protestations of loyalty, once the Wall fell she was quickly and conclusively lured away by the seductions of Ku-Damm.

Warring quietly with one another from their inception, each half of Germany, West and East—like the opposing sides in the forty-year Cold War—worked hard to mold its resident population into a distinct and cohesive nation. It is clear that the West won this battle. Of its own volition, the socialist state is disappearing. The "nationals" in its evanescent territory are now expected to subsume their identities under West German structures. East Germany is nullifying itself in a civic, democratic *Götterdämmerung*.

Through the biography of Frau Erika Gruner, I shall explore in this chapter how one East German—a loyal servant of the state—developed her identity and sense of self in fundamental opposition to many of the state's norms. Her story illustrates a basic failure of the state to create an active and valid community among its people, even among those who should have been its most integrated members. It was a failure peculiarly reinforced by the labyrinths of German history. Shifting loyalties and transient territoriality mark that history, a tale of fluid borders and impermanent governments.

Frau Gruner has lived in five Germanies in this century. Rococo and pretentious, gilded and reeking of gunpowder, the Berlin wherein she was born in 1912 was the capital of the meretricious Second Reich, ruled by the last Kaiser, Wilhelm II. As a young girl, she grew up in the Weimar Republic. She spent her early adulthood under the Nazi Third Reich. In this decade of death she was repeatedly imprisoned. Under the postwar administration in East Germany, her radical sympathies found free play as she worked toward restructuring society. She later became a judge and law professor in the German Democratic Republic. Even in retirement, change dogs her. As her state disintegrates, she will be absorbed into a new pan-German state modeled on the current Federal Republic of Germany. This remarkable woman has experienced high capitalism in authoritarian and liberal democratic states; wartime capitalism in a fascist state; the Cold War in a self-proclaimed socialist state; she will now live out her remaining years in a late capitalist liberal democracy.

Beneath her story, then, runs an outline of twentieth-century German history. Outwardly serene today, she has in fact been molded by the turbulence of that history: the political debates of Weimar, Nazi persecution, the *Stunde Null* of 1945. It is important to understand how Frau Gruner sees herself in the context of this history. Knowing her perspective, we can see what the political movements of the century meant on the level of ordinary life, as well as the reasons why Frau Gruner long perceived the division of Berlin and Germany as a possibility rather than a tragedy.

THE EDUCATION OF A RADICAL

My acquaintance with Frau Erika Gruner goes back to the early spring of 1987. I was doing research in Berlin on the relation of autobiography to legal and political history. My adviser at the East Berlin Humboldt University held the Chair of Family Law, Professor Anita Grandke. One of her assistants, an expert in custody law, Dr. Ilona Stolpe, was assigned to me for daily advising and was of great help to me. Among other things, she arranged for me to hear the life story of Professor Gruner, who had held the first Chair in Family Law at Humboldt before she retired.

"Herr Professor Borneman," Frau Doktor Stolpe warned me, "be on time. Professor Gruner is getting old."

About two hours into our first meeting, in response to a question about what happened to her after the war, Frau Gruner broke off to speak in hushed tones, with far more intensity than before.

"I haven't told you yet that I fought against fascism, from the hour of its birth on. Later I was arrested and sentenced to prison for preparing a protest. I sat there for one and a half years. I was released, but I remained a very special *Liebling* of the secret police. My movements were followed, I was persecuted on all sides, and yes, twice more I was arrested—they rounded me up" (she laughed) "whenever the Hitler regime felt itself endangered. I never thought I would live through this period. It was an unimaginable experience, the Eighth of May. That was really a gift without comparison, to have survived this horrible time."

For Frau Gruner the 12 years of Nazi persecution and the final liberation of Europe from fascist bondage, on 8 May 1945, were the essential, formative experiences of her life. Everything that happened before—and perhaps all that happened after—pales to bland insignificance against those years of terror and danger. She is a member of the "Victims of Fascism" organization and regularly visits local schools to speak to children about her experiences under the Nazis and the nature of fascism.

Her whole early life seems to her, in retrospect, merely a period of training, albeit inadequate and blind, for the anti-fascist crusade.

"I grew up in a family of skilled workers. My father was a metal worker, politically active in the trade union and in the Social Democratic party. My mother was a seamstress, and was also politically active. They were both involved in the Free Thinker Movement, an atheist organization that split from the church. [They] had already begun their political activity before the First World War."

Frau Gruner was raised with a consciousness of a separate, if still only nascent, working-class culture that stood in opposition to the regnant bourgeois norms. Socialist organizations throughout Europe were developing rituals and ceremonies to affirm the distinct identity of the proletariat.

"My mother," Frau Gruner recalls, "took part in the first *Jugendweihe* [the celebration marking passage from youth to adulthood] in Germany, here in Berlin, in the same house where I had mine. [It] wasn't a Christian youth confirmation, but an atheist one. [Mine] was organized by the local SPD on November 18, 1926, on the same day as we celebrate the [Russian] November Revolution. It was quite unusual back then.

"I've always been an avid newspaper reader. My father had a subscription to *Forward*, the SPD paper, and I always read the cover article. My mother subscribed to *Equality*, a women's magazine edited by Klara Zetkin, which I also read." Klara Zetkin was a feminist, a friend of Rosa Luxemburg, and a Communist member of the Reichstag. In 1933, as the oldest member of Parliament, she had the privilege of giving the opening address to the last group of representatives elected democratically under the Weimar Republic. In that speech, she vowed to resist the Brownshirts and never to give up her fight for communism. Shortly thereafter, Hitler had a dictator's power at his command. The Communist party was banned and Zetkin died within the year.

"Late at night when I heard my mother coming, I'd quickly put the candles out; I was supposed to be sleeping and not reading.

"Back then there was theater for common folk, called *Rosatheater*"—red theater, drama for the proletariat—"and we used to go there, where they had concerts for us also." (The Communist party in Berlin had an active cultural program to "raise the consciousness of workers" through a combination of artistic and pedagogical resources.)

From an early age, Erika saw discussion as the great good: freedom for her meant the freedom to speak, think, contend, mold words into sentences manifesting a liberated self. Indeed, one of Frau Gruner's first memories of gender discrimination was of a time she had been silenced.

The most astonishing experience," she told me, "was when I was fifteen or sixteen. It involved a personal discussion among my relatives. My father and uncle were discussing the strike situation, and talking about the tactics used by the SPD and KPD, and I was interested in that, and listened in. I risked asking a question. 'What's that?' They certainly didn't want that, that I should ask a few questions in between. 'Go back to the women,' they said to me. I would back away a few steps, be real quiet, and then go back again. That was the very first time that I noticed men and women were treated differently."

For all her proletarian roots, however, Erika was also steeped in high, bourgeois culture. "We also had books to read at home, for example Dostoyevsky's *Crime and Punishment*, which I read when I was ten; and it influenced me greatly. The penetration into the depths, the possibilities for seeing life!"

She attributes to the intensely psychological and introspective tone of the novels she read some of the interests that led her eventually to become a judge. "Later I always tried to penetrate beneath the surface of people's behavior, to ask about their motivations and purposes."

It is hard not to see Frau Gruner as suspended, even at that early age, between the cultural identities of different classes, between the emergent, indigenous properties of the self-assertive working class and the ambience of nineteenth-century novels. The cultural property of the middle class, these novels were already being co-opted by mass culture, though a future generation of Socialist Realists would call them "bourgeois literature." Whether or not she was conscious that her precocious range of interests and voracious reading habits were setting her on a different track—as a budding "intellectual," not cut out for manual labor—from her proletarian peers, she was already developing a critical capacity and a skepticism that would perceptibly affect the nature and intensity of her future commitments, political and ideological.

The ambiguity of her position reflected a general problem with working-class movements which tried to develop a resistance-consciousness in the alienated. Their pronouncements tended to be borrowed from the pronouncements, sophisticated, eloquent, or direct, of the bourgeoisie.

It was an ambiguity suspended between two classes, reinforced by Frau Gruner's education.

"At that time I was in a public school with religious instruction, which was obligatory for us. I've always had doubts about religious instruction, and shortly thereafter I had the opportunity to go to one of the New World Schools. This type of school was created by the bourgeoisie to give children from the petite bourgeoisie the chance to learn and study, so that their potential for the capitalist society wouldn't be lost."

This ardor for integrating the dispossessed into a system of possession was played out in peculiar ways, however. It created an educational system caught in cross-purposes, unsure what it was training the lower classes to *be*. Furthermore, control of the education policy in Berlin during Weimar was strongly contested by the Communists and the Social Democrats. Both wanted to reach and teach working-class children. The Social Democrats aspired to make these children competent to live in a capitalist world, albeit a more humane and democratic one: the children would remain loyal to their accustomed station, but learn the "habitus"—the tools, life-ways, dispositions—of the bourgeoisie. The Communists wanted to radicalize the children, instilling in them a class-consciousness and a desire not to reform but to transform the system.

"In Berlin, we had a Social Democratic school administration that placed particular value on educating working-class children. It was hoped these children would later, in their occupational life, continue to represent their class of origin. Of course, this viewpoint didn't work quite this way in practice. Class consciousness—that word wasn't even used by the Social Democrats—didn't even come up in our instruction.

"I had heard about the establishment of these World Schools, and told my mother about them. There was one a bit of a trek from where we lived in Berlin-Neukölln. I was thirteen then, and ready to enter a school that prepared one for the *Abitur* [college entrance exam].

"I always had a rebellious spirit, and I wouldn't let anything please me." Frau Gruner reflects on the origins of her own critical intelligence. "My mother told me that I couldn't get any support from home to go to this school. My father was often unemployed. He was on the Black List because he had gone on strike. And when times got tough, he was the first to lose his job. Things weren't going well, but still I thought I might get a small grant. I said to myself that I'd give up all those things that were important to girls my age. That stuff didn't concern me—I wanted above all to learn."

Finally, she achieved her goal. "I was admitted into this new school and it was wonderful, because there the students were respected, their opinions were consulted, the instruction was relaxed. We were encouraged to do our own work and had so many possibilities. Most important were the expression of different opinions and the democratic education. The majority of teachers were members of the bourgeoisie, but they fit into the style there; the rest were Social Democrats, a few were Communists. Those that pleased me most were the Communists and Social Democrats with political goals they wanted to realize."

Idealism and social action on the one hand, a democratic and critical atmosphere on the other: these were the aspects that most impressed young Erika. The school was a curious mixture of working-class earnestness and a peculiar (highly bourgeois) academic liberalism, an isolation from practical necessities that supported the students in their adolescent explorations.

"In the school," she remembers, "I was a member of the democratic administrative board, which was an inspiration of the November Revolution. Actually, it didn't have an administrative function, for the school plan was already set." The school was by no means a democracy but the trappings of consultation, of dialogue between different levels in the hierarchy, were there and gave her a taste of the freedom to argue and disagree she never forgot.

There was also an atmosphere of privilege, of comfort, in this working-class haven. "We were allowed to plan our own vacations, and the school was always arranging large parties. Pedagogically, that was quite important, and we even got money for it, money we gathered from all possible sources. In our school it was essential that we learn to travel, first in Germany. Then at the age of sixteen I went to Prague, next Vienna, and finally Paris."

Frau Gruner's eyes lit up as she spoke of visiting these romantic cities like any bourgeois tourist, a right all-important to her in the 1920s, but denied her own children after the building of the Wall.

"French was my foreign language, and everyone in the French course was entitled to go. It was well organized: we lived in a school dormitory owned by the Communist party there—my teacher had good contacts with them. We went to the Louvre and saw all the sights.

"Now perhaps you understand," Frau Gruner observed, "why this school was so important to my life. Because of this experience, I learned to be self-reliant. It was more important for me than my family."

It was this virtue—an essentially bourgeois one, the capacity for independence and idiosyncrasy—that her education inculcated in her more than any other trait or skill. Though Frau Gruner's socialism (unlike Hildegard's) is no embrace of *kleinbürgerlich* stolidity, it is still articulated in terms that many in the capitalist West would find familiar, even comfortable. It is an intensely felt, almost luminous devotion to the common good, a position in which Frau Gruner, critical, intellectual, judgmental, still somehow manages to stand apart, a loner, an isolated observer.

From the beginning, her education as a proletarian endowed with *Geist* made her more an abstract thinker and an *apart*, unique person than a member of any identifiable community. It divorced her from her class of origin, the proletariat, yet made her skeptical of her new, "learned," class, the bourgeoisie. Perhaps this was inevitable. She grew up in a Germany where any social movement, even one arising from the material privation of the most exploited members of society, had to accommodate itself to the demands of a deep-rooted *Kultur* and a tradition of abstract thought. Frau Gruner's socialism always exhibited a critical distance. She learned to be skeptical of any form of established wisdom.

PRELUDE TO FASCISM

Frau Gruner's engagement with her ideals and with working-class culture remained profound, however. "I was active in the school administration," she recalls, speaking of the shadow government the students were allowed to maintain. "In my final year I was chair of the school board. In that year we proposed renaming the school, and we chose 'Käthe Kollwitz.' "

Kollwitz was a Communist party member and visionary painter of great power in depicting the poverty and degradation of working-class life. She was one of the first artists to draw attention to the dangers of Nazism. After Hitler seized power, she was put on a black list and periodically interrogated by the Gestapo.

"I wrote Kollwitz," Frau Gruner says, "a letter asking if she would approve. Then I prepared a long speech for the renaming ceremony, but Kollwitz didn't want a big to-do. So I shortened the speech, and she came. It remained Käthe Kollwitz School until the Nazis came to power.

"After school we watched the great political confrontation with rising fascism, which was already underway, and decidedly underestimated. There were also fights between the Social Democrats and the Communists. I stood decisively on the side of the Communists, although my father was a Social Democrat. We discussed this passionately. I would take the cover article of *Forward* and point out to him everything that wasn't true. I was involved in the socialist school movement then, which meant going to school on the weekend, too. There we read Lenin's *State and Revolution* and selections from Rosa Luxemburg."

I asked Frau Gruner if she had been taught at the time about the differences between Luxemburg and Lenin. Lenin insisted that the major struggle was to wrest power from the hands of the bourgeoisie, by any means necessary, and to establish a dictatorship led by members of the working class. Luxemburg, the intellectual leader of the German Communist party in the Imperial period, argued that the proletariat must guarantee the democratic freedoms characteristic of liberal bourgeois republics: freedom of press and assembly, free elections, and freedom of opinion. Her famous adage, "Freedom means guaranteeing the freedom of those who think differently," was used by opposition groups at the Rosa Luxemburg Memorial Parade in 1988 in East Berlin to prod the aging leadership into instituting democratic reform. The Stasi arrested hundreds of protesters, claiming the citation was "blasphemy" against a Communist hero.

"We read Lenin uncritically," Frau Gruner replied, "and we read Rosa Luxemburg uncritically. For us their differences were fine points." Intricacies and contradictions were subsumed in the basically oppositional stance young leftists took. They defined themselves chiefly as against the bourgeois parties, hence internal disputes were secondary. This position (from which maturer leftists might have learned much) still gave free play to Erika's critical faculties. She was beginning to assert herself against the society she inhabited. "We learned the basic principle of [Lenin's and Luxemburg's] work: class conflict. I did my senior thesis on Trotsky, on the recommendation of the school principal, who, to be sure, had ulterior motives there.

"But we were not taught that she [Luxemburg] differed [from Lenin] in her opinion of the October Revolution. I did know that Lenin had called her an eagle, but I never knew why."

I asked Erika whether Rosa Luxemburg ever served her as a role model because she was a women. "That played absolutely no role in my case. I'm perhaps too abstract a person. I'm interested in historical standpoints, but the other details are not so important."

Whereas for Regine, Luxemburg was important in an almost savagely personal way, as a model and a sort of playing field on which Regine enacted her own private difficulties as an independent Socialist, for Frau Gruner,

Luxemburg was intellectually stimulating, not personally significant or totemic. Erika identified more closely with the broad view. Even "class conflict" begins to take on a rather abstract sound as she describes it.

Which is not to say that she was not personally involved in conflicts, some brutal and some heroic, merely that she was sustained in them by loyalty to an intellectual ideal, and to a community (a socialist democracy) not yet in evidence.

"More important for me," she says, "were the school board and socialist student movement, the student movement of the Socialist Worker's party [SAP], in which there were many Communists, and the discussions with my father, which I carried further in the school.

"This student movement led to discussion in the school, and we demonstrated together a lot. This was a time of severe class conflict in Germany. For example, on 1 May 1929, when the Communist party [KPD] was declared illegal, the demonstration on that day [in Berlin] was also forbidden. The KPD demonstrated anyway. There was a confrontation. The president of the police, a Social Democrat, stood there and shot at the demonstrators. That was in a worker neighborhood in Berlin-Neuköln—such a tense and heavily contested district. The workers erected a barricade on the street. The police shot at them from a roof— but the street was blocked so the workers couldn't escape. This wasn't very far from my school. The next day I went there with my fellow students and they were still shooting at each other. There were over thirty dead—killed by police fury."

These confrontations sharpened the conflict between the Social Democratic party (SPD) and the KPD. Both parties had been accusing each other of "social fascism"; in the end, they opposed each other more vehemently than they did the Nazis.

"The united front that was so necessary became really impossible after the shootings. The KPD always made offers for a unified front, but these offers came from the workers, not from the leadership.

"I can understand this perspective quite well from knowing my father, who hated the Fascists but also disliked the Communists. My father didn't want fascism, but in his eyes, the KPD was an organization intent on dividing. And he said that when they insult your leader, you can't make a united front. Later the KPD changed their course, but it was already too late to turn [the situation] around."

Frau Gruner did not join the Communists, however. In a typically idiosyncratic choice, she worked with the Socialist Workers party, a small splinter party of the SPD. The SAP stood primarily for a united front with the KPD against the Nazis. They were in essential agreement with the KPD about the nature of class conflict, the relation of classes to the state, and the desirability of socialism. Because the SAP wanted to work with the KPD, the Socialist Democrats rejected the SAP.

"We could see fascism coming," continued Frau Gruner. "Brutal street fighting, fear that the Nazis would mug you when you came home from an assembly. During this period I was very active, always doing something." Her recollections of activity always center around *discussion*, around open exchange of ideas, collective critical thought, argument and persuasion, the virtues of student life tenuously preserved in an increasingly oppressive environment.

"The offerings of lectures were so great during the Weimar Republic. I went to more than a thousand meetings:

the League for Human Rights, Friends of the Soviet Union, a group for decisive school reform. There was a society for homosexuals [run by the sexologist Magnus Hirschfeld] that hosted lectures, and I also heard what they had to say. All in the Weimar Republic!

"Then I passed my *Abitur* and wanted to study further. My parents preferred only the teaching profession for me. I said okay, I'll study history. But after one semester I totally switched—to business and law. That was at Friedrich Wilhelm University, as it was called back then.

"In 1931 the real misery began. I received a small grant from the Berliner Magistrat, and tuition was waived, but with the stipulation that I work at an accelerated pace. [On the side] I did all sorts of odd jobs, which were increasingly difficult to find. That worked until 1933."

When the Nazis took over, the decaying idyll of student life at last fell apart.

"I received a subpoena from the Berliner Senat, and they asked me if I had been involved in the student protests in February. I said yes, I'd been involved because I wanted to make sure the fascists didn't succeed. But then my time as a student was also up; a 1933 Nazi law forbade women to study. I'd already lost my grant, and I couldn't afford to study further anyway. The Senat was satisfied, and decided not to prosecute me."

THE DECADE OF DEATH

And then things become a little vague . . .

Under the Nazis Frau Gruner was reduced to doing "women's work." "I began to work in an office, really simple stuff. I hadn't yet learned to type. But I'd learned shorthand, that was enough. There I was first confronted with wage differences for men and women. I knew about it theoretically, but had to live it myself now, in praxis. A man in the office had about half as much in his head as I— perhaps I'm exaggerating, perhaps he had potential. But he was quite average in his ability to think, and his performance was so mediocre. Nonetheless, he got one-third more money than I. That frustrated me, I have to say.

"Yet as girls in the school and in the student movement we were absolutely equal."

The Weimar Republic had been a learning period for Erika Gruner. She became politicized and conscious of her allotted role as a woman from the working class. Toward the end of the Weimar period, she began to act on her beliefs, through demonstrations and political organizing, actively opposing the ruling coalitions of the state.

During the Third Reich, Frau Gruner came of age, married, and sought to live according to her political convictions. Those convictions forced her into open opposition to the Nazis, resulting in political harassment, periodic arrest, and imprisonment.

Frau Gruner does not like to talk about this period. One senses she is most comfortable discussing it in ritualized settings (as in her visits to schoolchildren), where it becomes a familiar and pointed tale to be told and retold, a story with a moral in which suffering is rewarded, if not with material goods then with social status, a story about good and evil, one that becomes its own justification, one that teaches its listeners something.

The truth is rawer, less "significant" even, in that it is less manageable, less reducible to envois and easy lessons. To preserve any integrity, any space in which she could resist, while living in a culture that has become murderous, is a labor perhaps incomprehensible to those of us who have not experienced it. Being critical is an absurdity in a criminal society; horror is a thing from which one cannot keep one's distance. Those who suffered, even in a small way, the onslaught of barbarity (and whatever the crimes of the Communist regime in the GDR, they are dwarfed by the omnipresent terror and monstrosity of the Nazi years) can be excused their silences.

Frau Gruner's life changed radically when the Nazis took power. For a long time the bourgeois bulwarks of *Kultur*— her parents' proletarian but profound cultural identity— and *Bildung*—her own educated freedom—had protected her, in a relatively serene cocoon, from the realities of working-class life. No longer. On all levels, oppression began to take on a personal meaning for her.

The end of the war and of Nazi rule was one of the most important events in her life. But the freedom it entailed— freedom to think and act again, rather than surreptitiously resist or impotently resent; freedom to recover her genuine critical distance—was imposed from outside. She did not have "the Germans" to thank for her liberation. The Russians had freed her from living in the Nazi state.

"You can't imagine," she says, "the extent of fear the Germans had of the Russians. More than a few people hung or poisoned themselves. Not only Goebbels, but also common folk. Our neighbor came home and found his wife had hanged herself and their two children. The women feared for themselves; they feared rape." But for Frau Gruner the apparent despoilers were rescuers. The Soviets saved her. It was her neighbors who had been her true foes.

Afterward, Frau Gruner never ceased to think of "Germans" as vaguely different from herself. Always a little detached from the classes about which she argued incessantly, never convinced that she was wholly proletarian, never remotely bourgeois in her heart, she became detached in spirit from the nation as a whole. Her relation to "Germans" and "Germany" has remained a critical one; "Germanness" was a flawed raw material to be remade, not an idealized *Ur*-nature to be recovered.

CREATING A SOCIALIST STATE

After the war, Frau Gruner worked with the Russian occupiers and later with the ruling Socialist Unity party to construct an East German socialist state, to reeducate the errant Germans. If during the Weimar Republic and the Third Reich she had identified herself as a nonconformist, in varying degrees of opposition to the German state, she was now a solid supporter of the new order. In 1949 the GDR was officially founded as a socialist state, a legal incarnation of the principles for which Frau Gruner had always fought.

In many ways she felt more at home than she ever had before, a feeling particularly bolstered by the new opportunities open to her as a woman, an aspect of her identity previously suppressed and silenced.

"German governments have always insisted that women's wages be less than men's," she told me matter-of-factly. "But it was different when the Occupation Armies came. . . . They passed an order [mandating equal rights] in 1946. It was like being hit by a bomb. It was particularly important to older women, who suddenly had a chance to learn a trade. This edict gave women unbelievable self-confidence."

"And the men," I asked, "how did they react?"

"How should I say it? It came from the Occupation Army. The Russians forced it on us. No German wanted to set forth the principle of equal work for equal pay.

"The Germans like to follow. My father always said, 'The party leadership, in the SPD, they'll already know what to do. Those that are above, they'll surely know better; they are, after all, educated people.' The Nazis very consciously cultivated this authoritarian behavior. Anyway, this edict mandating equal rights was issued by the military government in 1946. Women found it fantastic. Men went along with it. Those who remembered the Weimar Republic had an easier time of it; the others merely accepted it. It came from above. There were more important questions at that time, like how to survive, like how to overcome hunger."

There was still an element of detachment in Frau Gruner's attitude. She taught school for a year, but in 1946 her vocation in the new socialist republic became clear to her. She entered a special training program for judges. As a judge she could act and adjudicate at the very heart of the new socialist system, at the same time retaining a critical stance, sifting and evaluating evidence, looking with a trained and skeptical eye at the intimate daily life of society.

People from different social classes were admitted to the program, though the vast majority were from the working class. "Two of my classmates were miners, and they had such problems with studying. I helped them since it was all quite easy for me, having had some legal education before the way. A Russian came and gave us a lecture once. He said it was easy to tell right from wrong: 'Those who support you are your friends, and those against you are your enemies.' With that explanation, our miners were overjoyed; now they didn't have to read the old Civil Law Book in order to understand the law."

In 1946, Frau Gruner also joined the new Socialist Unity party (SED), the product of a forced merger of the Social Democratic and Communist parties. "People were surprised when I told them I wanted to join the party," she said. "They thought I was already a member." Her membership in the party, if not actually a precondition for becoming a judge, undoubtedly helped in her career.

She would probably have succeeded in any case, in a GDR desperate for officials untainted by the stain of Nazism. Command No. 4 of the Soviet Military Administration ordered the dismissal from the legal apparatus of all former Nazi activists. About 85 percent of the 2,467 judges, lawyers, and prosecutors in the Soviet zone were immediately dismissed. Most legal professionals of the Nazi regime fled to West Germany, which incorporated them back into the legal system after a 1950 amnesty. Those who stayed in the GDR were often prosecuted. One hundred and forty-nine were sentenced to prison there, whereas not a single Nazi judge in West Germany received a sentence. This purge of ex-Nazis in the Russian zone necessitated the immediate training and education of a new generation of legal functionaries.

"The legal system had been so neglected during the war, because they drafted so many lawyers into the service. And now we wouldn't accept those who had been Nazis. Not a single one," Frau Gruner says. "I could seek out the court I wanted. There were only a few people available for the administration of justice, including lawyers who retired before 1933 in order not to work with the Nazis, prosecutors who hadn't joined the Nazi party, and then refugees coming from the East who represented themselves as anti-Fascists."

Frau Gruner and her husband decided to settle in the city of Annenberg because it was mountainous and romantic. "My colleagues and comrades from my study group told me that I was crazy to go there. 'It's an area with nothing to eat. You'll have to leave your child with farmers, to make ends meet as judge.' That seemed exaggerated to my husband and me. We went to this beautiful spot—the largest circuit court in Saxony. They'd had seventeen judges with assistants before, but when I came, there was only one old lawyer, now over eighty, who agreed to volunteer for the legal work. On the very day I arrived, I had to begin work.

"I had so much to do, so many problems to deal with that I was never done. My most important task was to come up with a new criminal code. The people were literally driven to crime by hunger. I still see it that way.

"We received a new ordinance [from the Ulbricht regime]: The Protection of the Harvest. If this law hadn't been enforced, we wouldn't have had anything to eat. The people were going out with scissors and sickles, and cutting oats and digging up potatoes."

She tried to be fair, to take the ubiquitous suffering into account. "I did not treat everyone the same. Later we were told we had to differentiate [in enforcing statutes], but I did it right from the start," she says proudly.

Abstract in her ideology, she was precise and humane in its application. She realized that a good judge was not a mere technician of the law, making decisions in neat, regular rows—guilty! innocent! guilty! innocent!—and sentencing accordingly. She saw herself as a patient and exacting analyst of her society. Critical in the best sense, she considered details others neglected. She knew that the definition of a "crime" does not remain constant, that the delineation of an offense can be changed by circumstances, making the same action multivalent, sometimes punishable, sometimes innocent or even commendable. Her own "criminal" activities in the resistance during the Third Reich had convinced her that context was all in deciding the nature of criminality.

The law to protect the harvest gave her particular difficulty in determining sentences. "I allowed many people to go free immediately, but others I sentenced. The thing is, I didn't know what penalty to give out; I had absolutely no idea." She was allotted two lay assistants, *Schröffe*, with decision-making powers equal to hers. In an attempt to democratize the courts, the GDR allowed ordinary citizens to participate in judgment under the supervision of a trained judge.

"We had people from the Liberal Democratic party, who had been democrats already in the Weimar Republic, who were now working as my *Schröffe*. They had at least some experience with courts, and I could rely on them. A young man from the Ministry of Justice who had more experience than I did arrived there before me. I had no idea what should be penalized. My assistants promised to help me, and the man from the ministry said we would wait to see what sorts of complaints I got, and then I could make adjustments."

As she speaks, the excitement of this brave new world, in which law was being made and remade daily, comes back to her; for a moment the GDR is again a virgin state in which does and norms are still inchoate and she is ready to do the shaping.

"That's how I managed, although it really is complicated

to find the correct penalty. I see it the same way today. It's all so dependent on the environment, both the objective and subjective aspects. To find justice is not simple."

Frau Gruner stayed in Annenberg for one year. In 1949 she transferred to Plauen, west of Karl Marx Stadt. "Plauen had their own little, independent court back then. I had the same title there.

"For the first time I dealt with marital problems. I also handled some criminal law—there was so much smuggling [to West Germany] then, for example, of carpets made in state-owned companies, of music instruments."

Frau Gruner emphasized that she refused to take part in political trials aimed at punishing people for unorthodox beliefs or for supposed disloyalty to the state. Yet given the political climate in the GDR, she was invariably under pressure to turn "lesser crimes" into greater ones. When I asked her how she resisted this pressure, she offered an example.

"Once I got a complaint from the prosecutor that was incompletely prepared. Some very important things were missing. It listed [in the complaint] the objective part, what had happened, but not how the accused had taken part, what his intent was, and such things. The case had to be filled out. I first want to get a picture of what happened, and not to judge. The accused was charged with carpet smuggling; the evidence was really thin. I told the prosecuting attorney that it wasn't sufficient."

This demand for precision and completeness was her defense against the political pressure to impose exorbitant penalties without evidence. She enforced the rules of the emerging Stalinist system, but only in an *exact* or narrow interpretation. "Back then I was very devoted; I took everything seriously and wanted to be exact."

Frau Gruner dealt with the carpet smuggler's case by transforming it into a socialist theatrical, a public ceremony of communication and consultation. Instead of the rush to judgment the prosecutor wanted, Frau Gruner (rather like a soberer version of Brecht's Azdak, in *The Caucasian Chalk Circle*) envisioned justice as a spontaneous drama, emerging from dialogue. She literally turned her courtroom into a spectacle.

"Our court was in a large hall with a stage [the regular courthouse had been destroyed during the war], and on the stage we built a platform with a table for the court. Since the evidence was so thin, I said I wanted to speak [to all the spectators]. I walked down in front of the platform; the hall was full of blue collar and white collar workers from the [carpet] company. And I explained to them why this trial was necessary. That we couldn't allow this to go on. The carpets are our property, and they are our livelihood. I told them I couldn't imagine that somebody in the room hadn't observed the events being questioned, the smuggling in the plant. And I pleaded with them to help. Then I talked a little more softly, and they began speaking up, one at a time. Then I asked them if they'd say that as witnesses. They agreed to. I went back behind my judge's table, and called on the witnesses, and gathered enough material to complete the trial."

She remembers the continual compromises and consultations necessary to work out her vision of justice. "That was all very difficult for me. Often I had to function as a psychologist. I was unbelievably weak, very poorly fed. I was suffering from edema due to hunger. My fingernails had to be pulled out. When I had to sentence people, I could do it in good conscience, for I was living under the same conditions as they were. Had I had a full stomach, I couldn't have completed my tasks with a clear conscience."

The devastations of the war caused shortages everywhere. Peacetime was a cutthroat scramble for the shrinking reserves of basic goods. "It was really a warlike situation. This was also the time of the land reform, of expropriations. And people came to me, the landowners, who believed that they could win their land and property back by offering me something. These things were not problematic for me; I say this only to give you a sense of the atmosphere in which I worked.

"At this time I also handled marital matters. During the war, divorce requests had piled up. I looked into the records. You know, never before in my life had I seen such dirt. How married couples could throw dirt at each other! It was really instructive. I never experienced that before. It was so bad."

I asked her whether this had always been so, or if divorce had become more common and more acrimonious in the new Germany.

"Probably it was always that way. But this was the first time I had been exposed to such dirt. I dealt with the old requests quickly. Some of them concerned men who had died in the war, some of them men who'd gone West. There were the divorces of people with property—and precisely the bourgeoisie and petite bourgeoisie were those I had mostly to deal with."

She enjoyed the work, however, feeling that she was conducting a searching examination of the whole society. From her perch high on the dais, on the stage of justice, *she* was the audience, watching and absorbing the norms and habits of each class while remaining disinterested and equitable.

"There were many new divorces when the soldiers returned from the POW camps. I enjoyed handling new
problems, and I enjoyed dealing with the people, speaking
with them. I talked with them according to what kind of
people they were. I also had to talk with the defense attorneys sometimes, who often used old bourgeois manners
instead of talking directly to the people. I dealt with people
from the country and common folk. People from the country were more stubborn, rigid, as is rumored about people
from Plauen. But I still got along well with them.

"I can remember, twice I protected the husband [in cases
where the wife complained]. A woman complained that her
farmer-husband had wallpapered the walls of the house
wrong. She really just wanted to get rid of him. He had
served in the war and had just come back. He was a little
phlegmatic, not very decisive. The woman kept interrupting him, so I told her my opinion about how one should
deal with other people. Once I had to get really tough with
the woman—and finally I didn't agree to the divorce.

"But the most beautiful experience—a really beautiful
experience for me—was a married couple, who had been
married for eighteen years. The man had been in a prisoner-
of-war camp, came back, and now worked as a policeman.
The woman was a common worker, from a poor family.
They had hired a lawyer to get a divorce, because the marital relationship wasn't working anymore. The lawyer
pushed his points very aggressively. During the proceedings the husband made such a surreal impression, sitting
there silently. I asked the lawyer if he would please leave
the court for a few minutes, so I could be alone with the
two parties. He had insisted on interrupting, and kept
maintaining, 'My client wants . . .' and 'They would like a
divorce.' So I asked him to leave, something that isn't in

accord with normal court protocol—I knew that. I said, 'Leave me alone [with them] anyway, or else I'll break off the proceedings and recess.' Well, anyway, I insisted. He wanted to stay in the court. But I remained seated, and after a while he got up and left.

"When he was outside, I talked with them, with the wife above all, and I said to her that she should be patient with her husband, that he had lived through some very difficult times. Then I spoke very patiently with him. And I said to the woman, 'You know, you have a son who is seventeen years old, no longer a child, but still someone who needs both parents. Do you really want to break apart this relationship? You don't have another.' And her husband made a very good impression. Anyway, I said, 'I won't continue on today; I'll recess. But if you are still agreed that you want to continue, then please come back and ask for another appointment.' That was it. The woman was quite happy. The most beautiful part was that a month later I met the pair on the main street in Plauen. Walking arm-in-arm, they greeted me. That was a real joy for me."

Probably every divorce-court judge has just such a sentimental tale to tell, an idealized story of families reunited, of a wise word from the bench weaving two hearts together again, almost redeeming the whole messy daily round of mud slinging and broken marriages. For Frau Gruner the tale has a special meaning. It is a paradigm of her work as a judge, which she likes to see as integrative and constructive. From her bench, she was presiding over the making of a new, socialist community.

The sense of community was still important to her. She joined more organizations than ever. "In 1947 I had joined the Democratic Women of Germany [DFD]. That was still during the time I was learning to be a judge. I also became a member of the organization for 'Victims of Fascism.' Because of German responsibility for the war, there were enormous problems marshaling support for this new organization. Aversion was strong, for obvious reasons.

"I was active in the Plauen DFD, the second assistant in my district, and I really did a lot there, especially concerning equal rights. I gathered a large circle of interesting women and created an evening school. We discussed the book by the nineteenth-century socialist August Bebel, *The Woman in Socialism*. We found that book in a closet of the DFD headquarters. Otherwise we wouldn't have known what literature to read, but there it was. And what a gold mine for me, to be able to do evening education with this book. We met evenings after work, about five o'clock in the office of the DFD. And we had problems providing for them all—I had to do it alone. They were interesting women, all young, all learning for the first time, really, about the position of women and equal rights. I was the assistant to the chair, and was responsible for women from the proletariat. I had the job of making sure the events were well attended, and that things were carried through to their end. Our chair was from the Liberal Democratic Party. She owned a printer and had many contacts with women in the neighborhood and from her class. We worked well together. It was a wonderful thing.

"We discussed equal rights, women in the present society—and through this discussion I brought up the entire past: the Weimar Republic, fascism and why it happened, above all the role of property, what it means to create socialist property."

These and other meetings allowed her, as it were, to explain the distinctions she enforced as a judge, in an open and easy environment. The abolition of private property was particularly difficult for many to accept. Private property had ceased to be a category under GDR law. Instead, three forms of property were recognized: socialist (*volkseigenes*), communal (*genossenschaftliches*), and personal (*persönliches*). Socialist and communal property were held in common trust for the people, and were centrally administered. Personal property resembled private property in bourgeois societies, but could not be freely bought and sold. Moreover, only certain people (a narrowed definition of family) were allowed to inherit personal property.

"Our events were always well attended, above all by men. The people were excited to discuss the overthrow of fascism. Anyone who thought about it was encouraged to ask the questions that moved him. For example, when we discussed the position of women, we stayed up until midnight. First I gave a short speech, then questions followed. Immediately they asked questions. It was so satisfying for me that the people were really with us. They didn't want to hear any prepared lecture, but rather the answers to their questions. And it was the kind of event where they got answers." She reflects ruefully on how these answers somehow didn't last, on how people ceased over the years to believe them. "Perhaps I oversimplified too much, when we look at it from today's perspective."

In later years, Frau Gruner served on the national committee of the DFD in Berlin. "I would travel to the other districts and listen to their events, but they weren't very lively anymore. They went too much according to a model, not like our style in the beginning. In Plauen we had a March 8th celebration in the theater with several speakers. I would speak without notes, but concretely, holding to the essential points.

"I met a woman from the Plauen school board with

whom I am still friends today. She'd brought someone along, from the Federal Republic. They both said that my lecture was very instructive for them. On 10 October 1949, as our constitution took effect, I also spoke at a gathering in the center of the city [Plauen], in the name of the DFD, and within minutes the people came to hear. It began to rain, and I thought, God forbid, when everyone gives their two bits, from the political parties and the trade union, it won't work. But we did it.

"Back then everything was, how should I say it, more individual. You could get more of your own ideas across; that was encouraged. People were hungry for new ideas. Anybody who had any could do something. Later everything was overorganized, and you were supposed to hold to a prefabricated format. But I never gave up speaking freely. And it worked out well for me. I managed to bring my professional, personal, and societal activities together."

Frau Gruner was commissioned (in 1951) to complete five months of intensive study in the law, during which time she had to leave her husband and daughter. When she returned, she received a telephone call from the Minister of Justice, Hilde Benjamin, "Red Hilde," sister-in-law of the late Walter Benjamin. The minister asked Frau Gruner to transfer to the district court of Dresden. Although she and her husband were happy in Plauen, they agreed to go where she was most needed.

"Only a few comrades worked in the Dresden court. Most of the judges were older, the Chief Justice also. The Dresden court also had women who had studied law in the Weimar Republic, but couldn't practice during the Nazi period. Back then not every court had a comrade." The Honecker regime later extended party control more fully over the justice system. By the 1980s there were few non-party members sitting on the courts.

"I was first assigned to deal with civil law, and had to learn how to make judgments corresponding to the rulings of the Supreme Court. But I also had to make sure the opinions were in touch with the needs of the time. We were still working with the old Civil Law Book from 1892. But now we had the new constitution in 1949, and we were in a unique position in that we were allowed to apply it directly ourselves, in order to regulate the old civil law. We were, then, in this absolutely creative phase; we didn't yet have a new family law, civil law, and so forth."

They were reinventing the law as they went on, remaking it on the model of the old forms of legality, but changing it to correspond to the concrete needs and practices of the people who came before them. "We had to work out of the praxis which corresponded to our new historical position.

"I did civil and family law, later also criminal—traffic and economic violations, labor law. I never took part in political processes—processes against Nazis and war criminals. With labor law, we worked on inheritance, the rights and duties of renters. We had to break with the principle that the landlord had sole control over rent prices. In family law, we had to change nearly everything. For example, there was the so-called 'defloweration entitlement.' If a man broke his engagement with his lover, the woman had the right to insist on holding him to the marital agreement provided she could prove she had been deflowered by him. Then he would have to marry her. We fought with the older judges who insisted this was an important advantage for the woman, that we shouldn't sacrifice it just to enforce the equal rights provision in the constitution."

It was perhaps the arguments, the opportunity to review the past and present of society with a critical eye, that most excited Frau Gruner. "In our discussion we had to review the entire history of the thing. And that we did with pleasure."

THE TRIALS BEGIN

"As a judge, I was in a politically sensitive position. and when I said that I wasn't in agreement with what they were doing, one day I was suddenly forced out, I was fired."

By "they" Frau Gruner means the party's Central Committee. "That was the time of the [uprising of the] seventeenth of June, 1953. The Soviet occupation forces were here, and they had a very strong influence on our political development. Ulbricht was fully prepared to carry out their policies. That means Stalin's course was followed here, something we do not eagerly acknowledge. We've paid dearly for the errors that have been made by our leadership."

Frau Gruner said this in 1987 (and while describing these experiences, she asked me to turn my tape recorder off: "We're not that far here yet," she exclaimed). In the end, of course, the price was even higher than she had imagined: a total negation of all the political leadership had tried to accomplish, and ultimately the dissolution of the state.

The June 1953 uprising was stimulated in part by new, draconian measures against pilferage. The workers' and farmers' state was turning its strictures against the workers themselves. "That was the remarkable stupidity of the leadership back then, in 1953. They passed a law [to protect socialist property]. But how absurdly they proposed to protect it! It was intended to defend socialist property [*Volks-eigentum*] but they hadn't reflected on the class situation here. In fact, the Soviets had forced it on us. Willi Stoph, the head of the trade unions, who knew the workers, tried to persuade them to change it, but the Soviets wouldn't allow that. So he went along. I know that [Minister of Justice] Benjamin had second thoughts on the matter. She was skeptical, but she went along anyway.

"Every single person on the street has a stake in socialist property. At that time over sixty percent of the industrial property was already nationalized, and many people were working in such industries. There was tremendous misery, and one person would take a bratwurst from their factory and another a loaf of bread. Naturally, little by little it adds up. In any case, socialist property was being damaged by this pilfering.

"The regime reacted, though, with terrible severity: whoever took something—even of minimal value, under ten marks [$4.00]—got a minimum of one year in jail. Can you imagine that? At home you had a grandmother with her grandchildren, and the mother would take a bag of groceries home with her from work. And for that she was put in jail for a year! "I couldn't enforce it. I always looked for a way out. Being a clever judge, I'd already learned a great deal, and would always apply other laws, laws not used by others. Our judgments were all reviewed by the authorities, and mine by the Ministry of Justice in Saxony. They were already aware of my opinions. On the one hand, my good opinions impressed them—Hilde Benjamin had even cited them positively in her own publications—and on the other hand, at this time I suddenly was singled out for my mistaken judgments."

There were other lapses from ideological purity in her

record. She was noted for her leniency in the political trials which multiplied in the early 1950s. Frau Gruner remembers one of these trials which came before her in the Dresden court.

"The official responsible for the case was sick or at a health spa somewhere. Anyway, I jumped into the case. It was really hot, this story, and the accusations were all overblown, really trifling matters. Other motives were behind the case. They wanted to get rid of this man—a comrade, Communist, and Spanish Civil War veteran who'd even lost an arm there. He had a doctorate in economics, and headed the *Verband der Konsumgenossenschaften* [a union of stores for consumer goods] in Saxony. After the Spanish Civil War, he'd gone to England, and from England to Yugoslavia in order to fight against German fascism from there. Everyone who came from Yugoslavia was suspect [after Marshal Tito broke with Stalin]. There were many waves of suspects, who were to be driven out of all responsible functions. And the trial was supposed to serve the purpose of getting this man fired.

"It was clear to me—for I didn't know about the Yugoslavia connection, I learned about that much later—that everything that stood in the complaint was ludicrous. Anyway, nobody wanted to handle the trial. Other judges were all so curiously unavailable. Then I received a letter from a comrade in Berlin, who said—I knew him well—he knew this man being put on trial, and he only wanted to say that he was a very honorable man. It was all very alarming to me.

"I had to convince my assistants [to go along with me], which I did. In any case, I came to the conclusion that it would be better for him if I didn't absolutely acquit him. Instead I'd convict him of something that actually hap-

pened, but was a trifle to him. He'd taken some coal without approval—at that time we had such shortages.

"I judged him on that minor offense; he was convicted,
and I suspended the sentence. The prosecuting attorney
jumped up as if he'd gone mad. My husband was watching
the proceeding and said he thought I'd be arrested, the
prosecuting attorney carried on so vehemently.

"However, the man wasn't released from prison [after I
suspended his sentence] and the prosecuting attorney appealed the decision. My judgment was voided upon protest
by the prosecuting attorney and the case was sent to the
Supreme Court in Karl Marx Stadt, where they thought
they could win it. There, no new evidence came out, and
the case finally fell under an amnesty. There were constant
amnesties back then, a continuous series, either for some
holiday or for the state's anniversary. The man was released. I met him later, and he didn't want anything more
to do with official functions. He had earned enough money
translating English historiography into German. But he had
been a wonderful organizer, a man who really knew how
economies function, a man who could have helped us a
great deal. And we didn't think we needed him!"

The moment of truth for Frau Gruner came at a judges'
conference in Saxony with 300 judges and prosecuting attorneys on hand. She became a victim of what was virtually
a ritual ostracism, the dark counterparts to the theatrical
rituals of socialist democracy she herself had staged earlier
in her career.

"Two people were singled out. I was one; the other was
a [female] judge who also refused to enforce the Law for
the Protection of Property. My legal opinions were attacked. Nobody there would talk to me. I was completely
isolated!

"During a break in the conference every person walked around me, and I stood there all alone. I don't even remember anymore if I said anything about it, but it would have made absolutely no difference. In any case, the country was in turmoil, and the courts were being restructured.

"That was all in 1953. After my judgment in the case [of the Spanish Civil War veteran], I received an order from the justice authorities in Berlin releasing me from my duties. I wasn't even allowed to enter the building where I had worked. Then they quit paying me."

As suddenly as she was cast down, she was raised up again—rehabilitated by mysterious and anonymous forces high in the GDR's inscrutable elite. A week after her release, Frau Gruner received a call from Berlin, saying that she could either return to her job in Dresden or choose another district court. "I ended up at the Supreme Court of Dresden, and later on the District Court in Dresden. I had important functions. The whole episode didn't damage my career."

I asked her why. "I suspect that I had a guardian angel in Berlin," she replied. "I never found out who that was, because there was never another incident where I was so discredited."

The episode sapped her of something, though, both of her faith in the leadership of the new socialist state and of a measure of initiative. She could no longer calculate with confidence which of her actions would be applauded and which would be disdained. The state allotted punishment and reward by unwritten standards of its own, arcane and unintelligible to its servants and to the baffled citizenry as a whole. There were higher judges busily judging Frau Gruner, and there could be no dialogue with them, any more than with a *deus absconditus*. The whole process of

FIGURE 1: A West German map of "Germany" from the 1950s. From left to right: the Federal Republic of Germany, the Soviet-occupied zone of Germany, the territory under Polish administration east of the Oder-Neisse Line, and much of the Ostgebiete, which is under Polish and Soviet administration. The legend reads: Shall this situation continue? No! Never! Reunification in peace and liberty!

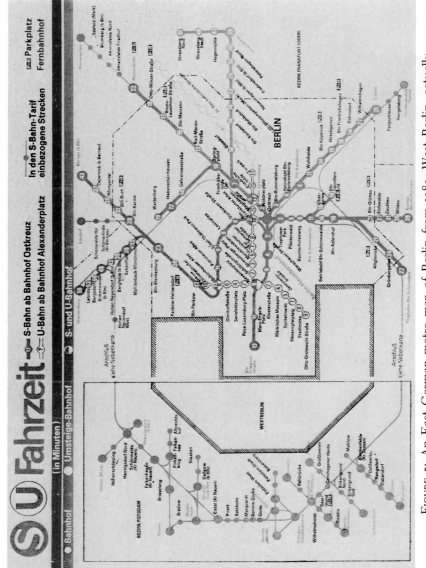

FIGURE 2: An East German metro map of Berlin from 1989. West Berlin, actually

FIGURE 3: The building of the Wall in 1961 divided Bernauer Strasse down its middle. The photo shows the division taking place from the West Berlin side. (Photo courtesy of German Information Center.)

FIGURE 4: The Wall in the 1960s, not yet fully constructed, with the East German slogan from that period: "Unity and Justice and Freedom." (Photo courtesy of German Information Center.)

FIGURE 5: Berliners chip away at the Wall on the evening of its opening. Pieces were later sold to Western tourists. (Photo by Martin Patek.)

FIGURE 6: The tattered Wall in front of Brandenburg Gate in April 1990, with East German authorities removing sections. (Photo courtesy of German Information Center.)

FIGURE 7: The two Germanies staged a united ceremony on 22 December 1989 for the official opening of two crossings at the Brandenburg Gate. West German Chancellor Helmut Kohl stands behind the microphone, with West Berlin Mayor Walter Momper on his left and GDR Prime Minister Hans Modrow on his right. (Photo courtesy of German Information Center.)

FIGURE 8: During the first three days after the opening, 1 million people crossed the Wall from East to West. (Photo courtesy of German Information Center.)

FIGURE 9: On 18 November, ten days after the opening, a store on the Muellerstrasse in West Berlin was already offering commemorative T-shirts, though the East German buyers seem more interested in *Damen Strumpfhosen*, women's nylons. (Photo courtesy of German Information Center.)

FIGURE 10: East meets West in the New Berlin. Several months after the opening, an East German guard peers at a West German tourist through one of the many new holes in the Wall. A third West German asks them to shake hands as he photographs their encounter. (Photo by Martin Patek.)

judgment into which she had thrown herself with such fervor suddenly seemed irrational, easily corrupted. Frau Gruner no longer saw herself as a true architect of the new state, but more and more as a passive object of history.

Even those GDR functionaries with major tasks and responsibilities tended to see themselves not as central members of an integrated community, a full-fledged nation, but as pawns of a process beyond control. Frau Gruner's sense of critical distance returned. She no longer felt the new German state was hers. The GDR was something she could comment on, even still judge, but could not fully participate in. During the Weimar period, when Erika had been summoned to account for organizing a political rally, even during the Third Reich when she was imprisoned, in all the crises of her life hitherto, she had bravely asserted herself, acknowledged her acts with pride. Now she became more and more private as her space for public articulation of difference shrank. She felt forced into silence and kept busy with technical matters and in administration.

She moved on to the District Court of Finsterwalde, where she lived during the week and visited her husband and daughters in Dresden on the weekends.

Frau Gruner's official duties always took a heavy toll on her family life. "My oldest daughter said to me recently, 'You know, I've first noticed it now, that Papa did everything for us and you weren't even around when we were children.' It's also apparent to me now for the first time, that I'd never have been able to take part in all those things if my husband hadn't been there.

"After four weeks in Finsterwalde, I received an offer from the District Court in Schwerin. My husband and I didn't want to stay around Dresden any longer. I wanted a different group of colleagues. But there were no apartments in Schwerin. I lived very provisionally, in a single room with a comrade whose husband had been killed in the war. Because the city of Schwerin was about an eight-hour train ride from Dresden—the Soviets had taken one rail from all the tracks, slowing down the train service considerably—I only went home every fourteen days."

Without an apartment of her own, she was forced to put her youngest daughter in a home for children during the week. After three months, "she was a totally different child," explained Frau Gruner. "Before, she had been such a happy child, laughing all the time. But now she was totally despondent. My husband came to see me and said we had to take the child back, we couldn't leave her there." He removed the girl and took her into his own care while living in Dresden.

After four months of service in Schwerin Frau Gruner was called to serve on the *Kammergericht* in Berlin. She wasn't sure she was up to the demands of the job, but finally accepted the offer on the basis of one overriding consideration: she couldn't get a decent apartment in Schwerin and was promised one in Berlin. The family could finally be together again.

"The court structure in Berlin," Frau Gruner remembers, "was the same as that under Frederick the Great. There was a Supreme Court of Germany and the Berlin *Kammergericht*, which should theoretically be at the same level as the Supreme Court. Actually, it was superior to it. The *Kammergericht* was the highest court of appeal for Berliners. Berliners were not subject to the Supreme Court's jurisdiction due to the Four Power Agreement— the Allies still had occupation rights in Berlin. The *Kammergericht* had both a civil and a criminal division. I was a judge in the civil."

In 1960, Frau Gruner became a junior professor of civil law at Humboldt University. After writing her dissertation, she was appointed to the first Chair in Family Law. Her memories of personal history thereafter become fewer and vaguer, as though time had become meaningless, trapped in molasses. I asked her if anything changed in 1972 when Honecker took over power from Ulbricht. She replied that there was "no revolutionary difference. Nothing decisive." Her disillusionment with the regime she worked for left her bored by its changes of window dressing.

"As a convinced democrat, I would have registered the difference, had there been any," she said, but it was more of a "style change" than anything else. The regime was still unable to deal with its continuing economic crisis and "get the situation under control."

THE SUMMING UP

After my stay in the GDR, I moved to West Berlin to do comparable research there. In late 1987, I invited Professors Gruner and Grandke, and Doctor Stolpe, to attend an introductory lecture on my research topic. Only Professor Gruner came. Professor Grandke had been denied a visa by the State Security—she was totally furious—and Frau Stolpe's invitation got lost in university bureaucracy in the East.

After the talk, I accompanied Frau Gruner in the S-Bahn, from Wahnsee back to Friedrichstrasse and the East. We quietly discussed Gorbachev's perestroika and the lack of response in the GDR. By chance, I had with me an interesting article from the Hamburger weekly *Die Zeit* on recent events in the U.S.S.R. As we neared the checkpoint,

offered it to Frau Gruner. She very carefully folded the
newspaper into fourths, compressing it into a small square,
and stuck the pages in an innocuous part of her purse.

How sad, I thought. How sad that this brave resistance
fighter, respected judge and law professor, dedicated servant of the East German state, should now fear carrying
across the border literature on reform in the Soviet Union.
How ludicrous that as a pensioner she should fear the
barely post-adolescent guards at the border, who, with the
authority of the state behind them, often meticulously
searched handbags to stop unwanted ideas from entering
their territory.

By the time we met again, in January 1990, the fear was
gone and the border itself was rapidly disappearing.

"You know that I've waited quite impatiently for these
events," Professor Gruner told me early in the new year,
less than two months after the East German regime had
caved in. We were sitting in her third-floor apartment on
the corner of Leninalle and Ho-Chi-Minh Strasse in East
Berlin. "The changes are coming four years late. If we'd
begun when Gorbachev came to power, then perhaps we'd
have had a chance. We are, after all, dependent on the
Soviet system."

The conversation had a surreal tone, as the old, committed Socialist assured me that the vicissitudes of socialism left her unfazed. "Altogether, I'm quite happy with
everything that has come to pass. But as someone who's
been through a lot, I do not, of course, see everything as
positive."

At the time of this interview, it was still unclear whether
the East German state would dissolve. Only three weeks
later, the pressure for unification overtook events, quick-

ening the pace of change and accelerating the total collapse of East Germany as a state and social system.

"I've lived through the entire history, from 1945 on, and
it's unimaginable with what enthusiasm we went at it all,"
she ruminated, "working to remove fascism from our lives,
and naturally, to build socialism. It was always my goal to
build a broad-based democracy. And in the beginning, it
seemed as if that would be possible. You were really encouraged to speak up. And over time, that became more
and more circumscribed.

"Back then we were all strongly influenced by our ideology—I was no exception. We all thought that we were
working for the construction of socialism. There were two
things we didn't clearly see: One was Stalinism. We didn't
see the extent of criminality there. And the other was that
we didn't understand what property was. Then, I should
add, the party had kept us busy."

Frau Gruner is still a member of the reorganized Communist party, although she supports the activities of her
oldest daughter and son-in-law in the opposition group New
Forum. "We have to break with the old apparatus, that's
clear. But it all comes down to: We don't want capitalism.
What we've had up to now has not been socialism, but a
centralized bureaucratic administration. At the same time,
the expropriation of the property of the capitalists has been
a positive accomplishment."

She continues to support the Communists because they
offer the only guarantee of socialism. "All the other political parties fear using the word 'socialism'; only the SED
still uses it. Central is the question of property, who controls it. What right do those who produce have? To say we
want either a plan or a free market is demagogic. Capital-

ism is planned also, intricately planned. But a real market can only be constructed when a state is qualified to regulate it."

She spoke abstractly, almost emotionlessly, of the rapidly changing situation. While she talked, I reflected on the many trials of her life, the ones she had suffered, the ones she had presided over; the struggles, the defeats, the occasional victories, like the Eighth of May. I mused on how all the changes, all the successive states she had inhabited, had never given her an identity that she could feel had a communal value. Caught between classes, she had defined her selfhood only in terms of opposition to the status quo. And when the promised socialist society finally arrived, she found herself cut off from taking full satisfaction in it. Like so many citizens of the state, she never felt she belonged to a true nation. She had invested her truest values in private longings. She was an exile, a displaced person, homeless despite her apartment and her respected position, despite her seventy-eight years of life on German soil, despite the dedication with which she'd served the land that claimed her.

"Many things are now surfacing that were previously repressed," Frau Gruner warned me. "Fascism is alive and well. And the SED has already lost thirty percent of its members." Frau Gruner said this in a humdrum tone, as if she had gotten used to the unexpected, even the horrible. She had just read about the desecration of several tombstones in the Jewish cemetery in the Weissensee section of East Berlin. On television she had watched a demonstration in Leipzig, where people carried anti-Communist banners, some with language taken from the Nazis. One banner read *Die Genossen in die Spree*, Comrades in the Spree, a phrase recalling how the Weimar Social Democratic regime under Friedrich Ebert had allowed the police to murder the two leaders of the Communist party, Rosa Luxemburg and Karl Liebknecht, and dump their bodies in the Spree.

The neo-Nazi slogans belonged to a numerically very small group of enthusiasts, numbering at the most 1,500 in the entire country. I asked her if she took seriously the SED claims about the threat these extremists presented. "Yes," she replied, and for a moment all the past came back to her, the years spent opposing the Nazis and the whole monolithic weight of German public opinion. Here alone was real satisfaction for her, in the memory of working *against*, not working for.

"In Leipzig, those were not young people who initially used Nazi slogans. It was the generation of former participants in the war. Looked at theoretically, it can't really be any different. Those people have never identified with the society here. Socialism was always something alien to them. And now they're overjoyed that their time has come. We can't allow ourselves to underestimate them." And she repeated, "You know, I spent time in prison under the Nazis. . . . "

On 14 December 1989 Frau Gruner took part in her first demonstration since 1946. It was a demonstration against neo-fascism organized by the United Left, a large coalition of mostly independent intellectuals and artists, and supported by the SED. It was held in the Treptow section of Berlin, next to the Soviet Memorial for fallen soldiers from World War I.

"There was a fantastic atmosphere. I took the S-Bahn to Treptow and couldn't get out—there was no more room to approach the Soviet Memorial from there. The conductors

wouldn't let us out; they told us we should go one more
station and get out at Planterwald. When we got out there,
only two people remained in the S-Bahn.

"The crowd was very mixed, with many young people,
but also many older married couples. We were unanimous
against reunification. People called out 'Nazis Out,' 'Never
Again Fascism.' [Gregor] Gysi [the new head of the SED]
spoke, and a man from the Liberal party was booed, so he
couldn't speak—that I didn't approve of.

"For me this was proof that the idea of 'anti-fascism' is
deeply rooted in our people. I remember in 1946 also attending a demonstration in Dresden for the expropriation
of property from Nazis and war criminals. Then, as now,
the people voluntarily came forth to march. That was important for me then, and this demonstration last week was
important for me now.

"You must remember that the most important experience for me was the Nazi period. I sat in prison in Prinz
Albrecht Strasse several times, always in isolation. I bear
the scars."

L'ENVOI

I talked for the last time with Frau Gruner on 21 March,
1990, several days after the election. She was not mourning
the collapse of the GDR or the victory of the Christian
Democrats.

"Disappointed," she admitted. Even "having to catch
my breath sometimes," she said. But she does not reproach
the state for its failures or herself for her years of service
to it. She seemed reconciled to the new situation.

She felt no overwhelming regret, knowing she could not lose what she had never had. "We never had socialism here," she suddenly asserted. "We couldn't have had socialism. I finally realized that when I went back to reading theory. Looking at it from a purely theoretical standpoint, it would have been impossible to have socialism under these conditions." She had been kept so busy with party meetings, with rewriting the old Civil Law Book, with creating new ordinances and new forms of "socialist law" that she hadn't had time to perceive this basic fact: she wasn't living in a Socialist state.

"We didn't have socialism; we had a form of state capitalism, a system of exploitation with a very few party elite on the top. A GDR type of capitalism dependent on violence for its authority; but also, at least, with a regime that paid some attention to the population. I am not saying that the GDR has no accomplishments. I can point to land reform, to programs to eliminate class conflict, to the creation of other forms of status groups, to the support given women."

"But Frau Gruner," I asked uncomprehendingly—for I remembered all her assertions of hope, her proclamations of faith in the final victory of socialism—"Frau Gruner, you wrote the Family Law Book here. You were a judge, you helped build the state, you initiated and defined many of these programs. Will nothing last? Nothing from the last forty years?"

She looked down and shook her head slowly, muttering in a quiet voice, "No. Nothing."

With those words, her moment of grief—at least as much of it as she would share with me—was over. She would speak no further of it. "My daughter," she told me, "who

was one of the founders of New Forum, feels totally devastated." The opposition groups responsible for organizing
the revolution had been crushed in the elections, by the
larger parties imported from West Germany. "She can't
face up to the defeat."

Suddenly Frau Gruner told me something she had held
back during our other meetings. "I was with her and the
others when they founded New Forum. I put up the
money so they could rent a hall for their first large assembly. And all along, I advised them to get rid of things in
their apartments that might harm anyone if found by the
Stasi."

Throughout the period of opposition, she had supported
her children and their spouses and friends, the next generation, in its long war against the regime for which she
had sacrificed so much. She had counseled them in their
legal rights, encouraged them with emotional and financial
support, knowing quite well that it might mean the elimination of all she had worked for. To the end, her admira-
tion for the critical, the oppositional stance remained
firm.

Now she assessed the future. "The market is coming,
and the full logic of that system will become our new proprietor. It is clear that we will be annexed, that many people here will profit from that. People starting from weaker
positions will do much worse. The career training in West
Germany is better than ours, and many of those who can't
find work over there will come here. That will make for a
climate of intenser class conflict.

"But as remembrances of the revolution, we have several accomplishments which will be with us for a while. We
have learned to respect the power of movements that exist

outside the established parliamentarian parties, that did not come together like normal political parties. These forms of protest and organization will last," she said, reflecting on the strategies and the years of struggle through which the the regime had been brought down. "I think they are necessary in any fight for justice."

6

Fantasy and Desire:
Images of the West
Beyond the Wall

"How can you sympathize so with the English? You don't even know English!"
"No, but I know German."

—Karl Kraus

A BIRTHRIGHT DENIED

Helmut and Marina were both in their early thirties when the Wall fell. Helmut called himself a communist, but was no friend of the regime. Marina, "very red" when young, had gradually lost her enthusiasm. She joined the SED at the age of twenty-one, whereas Helmut has never been affiliated with a political party.

Helmut's father was a conservative Lutheran minister,

his mother an apolitical housewife. When I first met him, his mother kept admonishing him to warn me about the dangers and evils of communism. She was afraid a naive American would be blinkered and deceived by the authorities.

"Tell him how bad things are here, Helmut," she'd say. "Tell him we live in a police state." Helmut never took it upon himself to remind me he was living in a police state, but he repeated what she said, always with a laugh. "My mother admonished me today to tell you . . ."

Yet Helmut and Marina's primary sense of the state seemed to mirror his mother's dire vision. They saw it as something to which they belonged against their will, an identity that set them apart from the rest of the world without offering much security or solace in return. They defined the state not in political but, essentially, in geographic terms. They felt acutely their separateness as GDR citizens. Division made them East Germans, or, as West Berliners say, "Ossies" and not "Wessies." They dreamed continually of the lost other half, like an amputee twitching his lost, ghost limb. It became a focus of fantasy and thwarted desire.

Opportunities to gain material experience of Western life were limited. The integration of West Germans and West Berliners into Western Europe, along with physical occupation by the Americans and the penetration of American culture into Western Germany, was known by East Berliners only at second hand, through television reports or visits from Western relatives, friends, or tourists. The physical presence of Americans was the only thing experienced directly, for soldiers from the occupation forces had the right to visit East Berlin without being stopped at the border. These uniformed soldiers, about half of whom were black, always stood out from the East Germans, not only in their clothing style, haircuts, and skin color, but also because they came to East Berlin to buy goods with money exchanged on the black market. Children's clothes, toys, and cameras were favorites.

As a doctor, Helmut ran into people from the other side in scientific conferences. I met him and Marina in November 1986 at such a conference in Rostock, a coastal city about 100 miles north of Berlin. It was sponsored by the GDR "Marriage and the Family Counseling Services." Helmut had been invited to give a talk on the reproduction of gender roles in preschool children. He argued that since the 1950s, little had been accomplished in eliminating gender roles in preschool children. Parents, including doctors, still raised children to behave like "proper" boys and girls. I overheard one of the organizers tell him, "Don't be so aggressive. Tone it down."

Since then, he has had increasing contact with scientists at international conferences, but these encounters are always shaped by his own early isolation within the closed borders of the GDR and by his intense consciousness of it as a lack, a default in his experience.

He remembers a geneticist from New York telling him at a 1989 conference, "You have a dirty mouth." Helmut was half-amused, half-angered. "I asked, 'What do you mean, dirty mouth?' The fat sow then said she'd never heard a foreigner speak English with such a command of cuss words. 'Do you know where I learned my English?' I asked her. 'From rock music.'

"And here she is, doesn't speak a word of German, comes to a conference in the GDR, and expects me, who essentially learned my English by listening to the radio station for American servicemen, to speak some kind of elite English!"

Helmut studied English for five years in school, but his instruction was not particularly good and, more important, he rarely had a chance to use it in practice. His self-consciousness about his idiosyncratic use of Shakespeare's tongue is something more than the awkwardness of some-one ill-at-ease with a foreign language. For English is more than a foreign tongue to him. He treats it as a language he *ought* to know, which he was kept from knowing by Ul-bricht, Honecker, the Wall. His troubles with it have be-come a synecdoche for larger frustrations. English takes the role of a mother tongue from which he was cut off by the barbed-wire-and-concrete erection that defaced his city. His bitterness reflects the ambiguous attitude of many East Germans toward a West desired for no better reason than that they lacked it for so long. Needs stifled in East Ger-many became focused on the West precisely because it was inaccessible, hence different from the hemmed-in self. Hel-mut feels paradoxically provincial because he hasn't mas-tered an alien speech he feels should have been his birthright.

DEATH BY TELEVISION

Marina came to have the same sense of being walled in, but came to it late. Much of her life was privileged, by GDR standards. Her parents lived in the country and worked in factories nearby. Many of her relatives are farm-ers. Marina studied to become an elementary school teacher, "not because I couldn't get accepted into any other programs," she explained to me, "but because I really wanted to teach and work with children." She found teaching frustrating but encountered no major bureaucratic or pedagogical problems until 1981, when she applied to work on a research project on the effectiveness of different teaching methods, sponsored by the Ministry of Education, headed by Margot Honecker, the wife of the head of state.

The problem Marina encountered lay in the security check necessary for the job. She had married Helmut, her longtime lover, the year before, mainly to expedite their move from Rostock to Berlin. Apartments were distributed by the state and they had higher priority for obtaining an apartment in Berlin as a married couple than as singles. Marina's application to work with the research project was rejected, because her husband was considered a security risk. Although her own family was "clean," Helmut had two siblings in West Germany, making both newlyweds suspect to the state.

"That was the first time I'd ever experienced discrimination," she told me. "Everything had been effortless for me before I married Helmut."

Marina continued teaching ninth grade for another four years. "And then I became completely fed up," she said. "Every attempt to be creative with the students brought me before the principal of the school. School authorities here are totally fixated on order."

Once, with Helmut's help, she had painted the inside of the classroom door red. Then, with an artistic flourish, she decorated it with a white question mark. The school director found it the next Saturday morning and repainted the door himself that very afternoon.

"Schools *answer* questions," he told Marina. "They provide *gesichertes Wissen*, secure knowledge. When you want to provoke questions, make sure you know what the answers are first." Marina decided she had to find a way out.

While doors were closing on Marina, new ones were opening for her husband. In 1988, Helmut was awarded a grant to write a dissertation as part of an interdisciplinary group working in the philosophy department of Humboldt University. Eager to have the time to write and read, he accepted a salary nearly half his usual earnings. He continued to practice medicine, out of a bad conscience, he explained to me, making house calls once a week.

Visiting homes in the evening became very important to Helmut. It opened up new worlds for him, ethnographic horizons, so to speak, for he entered into apartments of every conceivable sort. He joked about taking me along sometime so I could see for myself, since I am an ethnologist interested in how people live. Perhaps I could dress up as a hospital aide, he suggested, although (conscious as always of speech as a giveaway) I wouldn't dare say anything since my accent would betray me.

Yet the new worlds opening before Helmut were curiously arid, closed ones. He found that most of his countrymen lived stunted lives, bounded by the frontier of the television set. They barely noticed his coming and going, just pointing him in the direction of the sick person. In the evening they watched television—all of it West German, and always the same programs.

"I could go from house to house and follow the same story the entire night, never missing more than a five- or ten-minute scene in those stupid situation comedies on [the West German commercial station] SAT III. I swear those shows are made for idiots. I knock on the door, they let me in. Someone says, 'She's sick,' or 'He's sick. He's in there.' And then they sit down again in front of the television, having hardly taken their eyes off the screen to see who I was. It's real sad, John. And that's every night! They all have the television programs written out on some slip of paper so they know the programming ahead of time. I could do anything there I wanted to, and they wouldn't even notice me."

Until the Autumn Revolution, television programming was a major ideological battleground between the West and East German states. In the East, people were penalized in various ways if they were found to have watched West German television. In the 1960s, members of the Free German Youth organization (FDJ) went on punitive forays, breaking antennae recognizably able to receive West German airwaves. Children were asked in school about their parents' viewing habits: what shows Mummy watched, what radio programs Daddy listened to. If informed on by their children, parents were called in by the school principal and told their children would suffer the consequences for such inept upbringing.

The harassment and penalties simply drove the addiction to Western television underground, making it a covert, shameful, and all the more exciting activity. Thus, although watching television became more common in both German states as TVs invaded every home (in the 1950s in West Germany, in the 1970s in the East), in the East it took on a peculiar additional *frisson*, of the forbidden, the Other, the "free."

The West German state never worried about their citizens watching GDR television—for one thing, GDR programs were too boring to compete—and the East German state had no effective means of forcing their citizens to listen to their own propaganda. In the mid-1980s, the East German government relented. Admitting that the battle of the airwaves was lost, the state turned to a new, convoluted argument. Because its citizens watched so much Western television, there was no need to open the Western border. The populace was already amply informed about what went on over there. The government even agreed to build cables for residents in Dresden to receive West German programming. Dresden lies in a bowl that blocks Western airwaves. The difficulties in receiving West German television had contributed to making Dresdeners so dissatisfied that they had the highest rate of petitions to emigrate of any area in the country.

The Ministry of Culture also decided in the mid-1980s to show more American films in GDR cinemas, at the expense of Western European and especially Soviet ones. American big-budget films were known in the GDR for their depoliticized content. When they had a political message they painted characters in black or white, in stark tones with little moral chiaroscuro. The state found them useful in training its citizens to think in rigid terms; it was easy enough to reverse the sides later.

The state thus learned to use Western culture to pacify its own citizens. Far from exacerbating discontent, the opulent and exotic fantasy worlds that glittered inside the flickering TV—the mansions of oil-rich Ewings and jewel-laden Carringtons, the soap-opera odes to American wealth, all dubbed into German—encouraged passivity on the part of the enthralled watchers. The endless visions of extravagant spending furnished an imaginary supplement to, and distraction from, the trivial frustrations of daily life. The interchangeably lush serials and commercials both enforced feelings of inadequacy and inability to take effective action and offered a dreamworld into which one could sink by way of compensation. The invidious comparison (the realization that *I* could never be like *that*) was followed by the consoling retreat into fantasy (but one can always dream). In a small-scale anticipation of what happened when the Wall came down, the populace was fed brief, addictive glimpses of the inaccessible Other which both confirmed the sense of being second-rate, and provided a placebo for it.

Helmut and Marina, when they reflect on East German society, create a nightmare vision: a culture of diehard couch potatoes, invalid voyeurs. The anecdotes pour forth and reinforce one another; television has become a symbol for them of all the failures and neuroses of the national life.

Marina remembers the time she became pregnant with her second child. After giving birth to her first baby, she claims she was treated like a holy woman.

"For my parents, who, by the way, were quite hysterical about it all, both I and the baby were sacred, the most perfect creatures in the world." I asked her if that kind of worship had something to do with the social value put on giving birth in the GDR, with the importance of reproduction to a state constantly losing people to the West. She agreed that mothers, especially first mothers—93 percent of all GDR women have at least one child—are given a special kind of recognition just for having a baby.

The pedestal on which the second-time pregnant Marina was placed was a curious and painful one, however. During the last four weeks of this pregnancy, in early 1987, she suffered from a special condition forcing her to lie flat on her back in the hospital, legs spread and feet in stirrups. Instead of being the object of adoration, she was forced to adore the all-holy, all-high TV.

She shared a room with six other women, ineffectual and alienated whiners. "They cried all the time, but they never once got up to comfort each other. When one began crying, the response was, 'Let her cry herself out, she'll stop shortly.' One woman, who, after several miscarriages, had problems getting pregnant again, finally conceived, and had now reached her eighth month. All the other women were concerned that she might not carry the baby the full nine months. At first they all talked quite mystically about motherhood and their babies, and about how wonderful it was to be pregnant. But after I was there three weeks, this one woman, the one with the problem pregnancies, broke down and said she didn't even want the baby. She was only having it for her husband! Then the other women began saying the same thing, that their pregnancies were not joy rides. There was a lot of pain and sacrifice. And many didn't look forward to being saddled with a child for the next sixteen years.

"It was all very depressing for me. I was the oldest one there, at thirty-three, but they all treated me as if I were the youngest [and my opinion of no account]. The television was on all day long, but I didn't see a single newscast during that whole time. As soon as the news came on, they would change the channel. I asked them once, 'What would happen if New Zealand were destroyed by an earthquake? Nobody would know!' They answered, 'So what?' "

One of the ironies of Marina's story is that the Charité hospital where she was lying, located directly on the Wall in East Berlin, gets only Western television programs. In its location, reception for Eastern stations is extremely poor. Hence patients are limited to fighting over which West German programs they want to watch. Marina's roommates were quite happy, though. "Within a week I learned all the characters in the Dallas and Denver clans. They talked endlessly about *Dynasty*.

"An hour before the show, they would prepare themselves by repeating all the happenings from the previous show. One husband used to come to visit his wife nearly every day, and they would both sit silently the whole hour or two and watch television. Not a word exchanged about anything else. Then, when he was preparing to leave, she would say, 'But it's almost seven and in five minutes so and so will come on. Stay just a little longer.'

"One week there were two good films I wanted to see, *Mephisto* with Klaus Maria Brandauer and *Die bleierne Zeit* by Margarette von Trotta." Both films are critical of people who collaborate with a regime rather than fight for their ideals. *Mephisto*, based on Klaus Mann's novel, centered on a well-known actor who allowed himself to be used by the Nazis, ultimately so compromising himself that he could no longer distinguish his acting world from his real world. Von Trotta's film sympathetically portrays a terrorist motivated by moral concerns, whereas the state against which she fights (the Federal Republic) has no moral vision.

"With the von Trotta film," Marina remembered, "one woman said after the first half hour, 'But it is so boring!' And we had barely begun watching *Mephisto* when another woman said, 'Enough of this *Mist*!' And they all agreed to switch the station. I almost went crazy in there."

The women sought consensus. It was impermissible for anyone to express idiosyncratic interests that might rock group harmony. When Marina's interests differed from those of the group, she was given false alternatives to choose from ones that never included her own preference.

If there's considerable intellectual snobbery in Marina's

account, there is also vivid horror at an atmosphere of flattened-out, frightened victims, alienated and isolated in their fantasy worlds and completely dependent on the whims of the group.

Helmut happily chimes in with his matching story. At the age of twenty-five, he remembers, he spent six weeks quarantined with hepatitis in an all-male ward of the hospital. Two of the other men in his room were in their twenties and two in their forties. They argued incessantly and exclusively about what to watch on TV.

"Early on we collectively agreed to leave the TV on all day. We had a policeman among us, who initially insisted on watching GDR television, but he gave up after the first week. Soon he knew best of all what Western programs were on when, and he monitored them for us all. The other men? One was a logger, tattooed from head to foot; one was an acrobat with long hair and an earring. Initially everyone ridiculed the policeman—we called him Bull—a lot, but by the end of the six weeks, he had changed the most. All those attacks forced him to be more introspective, and ultimately he opened up more to us than we to him.

"The social hierarchy from outside broke down in the hospital when we all had to use a common potty. There was no toilet in the room and we were forbidden to leave our room for the entire six weeks. No guests either.

"We all agreed early on to make sex taboo as a subject, because we thought we'd go crazy if we started talking about it. The hospital administration was aware of this dynamic, so they sent only older nurses in to serve us. Once a week, though, a younger woman came in to take care of us. Every week she was more beautiful! First makeup, then high heels. Once she wore a red skirt with black underpants. She knew what she was doing."

It was all display. For the febrile, bedridden quintet of men life became a set of performances staged for them. The ward precisely encapsulated to Helmut the society outside in its reduction of the patients to an eager, immobile audience. As always, the best show was on the small screen. There they could watch the world beyond their four walls and beyond the Berlin Wall itself.

"One night we were watching a Marilyn Monroe film, and at the point where the camera very slowly zooms in on her breasts, the *Bulle* ended up leaving his chair and zooming in on the TV set until he was standing directly in front of it, on his tiptoes trying to look inside of it.

"You know, it could have been any of us," Helmut muses. For him, as for many Berliners, the Wall was less a stern edifice of stone than a blank screen, a glossy, empty TV surface promising pleasures that could never be touched. A physical barrier, in its very impenetrability it simultaneously served for 29 years as a gateway to fantasy, a field on which the trapped imagination played. The East Germans watching it became (to Helmut's cynical, observing eye) a nation of fantasists, of bedridden paralytics clutching for a remote control.

LORELEI

Helmut and Marina never did obtain approval to travel in the West, but they managed to obviate some of the isolation division brought about by establishing private contacts with Westerners through their work.

Hildegard similarly tried to render her confinement in the GDR less clouded by reestablishing contact with her husband's relatives. The effort backfired. The burden of fantasy and desire Hildegard brought to the encounters was too great. The result was only to intensify her almost neurotic feelings of inadequacy, jealousy, and frustration.

Hildegard herself had no relatives in the West. She had grown up as a Sorb (the Sorbs are a Slavic people currently represented by the Wends of Saxony and Brandenburg) in the tiny town of Bautzen, eventually a part of East Germany. Although many Sorbs cultivate a distinct language and cultural identity, Hildegard's parents did not. Her father taught secondary school. A soldier in the Second World War, he had deserted two months before the *Stunde Null*, hiding out in his mother's house. He joined the Christian Democratic party (then a satellite of the Communists) in 1949, and remains a loyal member today. Hildegard's mother, born to a farming family in Saxony, ran her own small farm for nine years before working alternately as cook and caretaker in a state-run day-care institution.

Hildegard grew up with some sense of a separate ethnic identity, but she always thought of herself as a German. Her father, like a good Sorb, raised her as a Catholic. During the early years of postwar state formation, the Sorbs used their Catholic identity as a basis of protest, resisting attempts by the regime to secularize their schools and customs. They resisted, for example, the institution of the *Jugendweihe*, the state coming-of-age, mock-confirmation ceremony. Yet Hildegard proudly took part in the *Jugendweihe* in her school.

"My parents always wanted me to do everything correctly," she explained.

All Hildegard's ties were to the East German state and soil. Her only childhood experience of the West was through a far-off, faceless figure of impartial largesse, a Frau Weidenhüller in the Federal Republic, who sent Hildegard's family packages every Easter and Christmas through the 1960s. Hildegard never saw Frau Weidenhüller and knew her only as "an idol figure, the personification of all that was good and generous."

The packages included coffee and "other good-smelling things, so that the good smell enveloped us even before it was opened." Her father would ceremoniously bring each box to his nose and sniff it, murmuring "hmmm." Then a ritual of gratitude to the unseen giver was enacted. "Who is Frau Weidenhüller?" Walburger's father would ask. The children had no idea. "But the package is from Frau Weidenhüller," the father would needle them. "It is she we must thank." He impressed on the children their responsibility to be grateful and dutiful. Frau Weidenhüller became a Santa Claus, a remote and mythical philanthropist whose name the parents invoked to sustain order. She was someone to be good for. Hildegard still takes a deep breath whenever she receives a package from the West, remembering "the warmheartedness of Frau Weidenhüller," this strange woman she had never seen.

Frau Weidenhüller was easy to fantasize about. There was no danger of ever actually laying eyes on her, of Hildegard's imaginary Weidenhüller-romance meeting with disenchantment. Hildegard's husband Bert enjoyed ties to the West that were firmer, more real, and more ominously prone to disillusion. Bert was always somewhat suspect in the eyes of the GDR. His Catholic parents had discouraged him from undergoing the *Jugendweihe,* a decision that hindered him in his career in the 1970s. He was less securely bound to the arbitrarily delineated homeland, with kin in three different states, East Germany, Poland, and West Germany. He could visit all except his aunt, in the West, but every other year, for a week, the aunt visited him.

It is one of the ironies of East German life before the Wall opened that citizens execrated the state for separating them from relatives they didn't like. The history of kinship in the two Germanies after the building of the Wall is one of continually reinforced inequality, humiliation, and deceit. Among the numerous inequities that made relationships across the border invidious—disparities in wealth, political freedom, access to goods and ideas—the fact that West Germans had a mobility denied to most East Germans ensured that jealousy and bitterness would mar the meetings.

Four months after the Wall was built, in December 1961, travel privileges were restored for most West Germans to travel East. Some travel to the West was eventually permitted East German citizens (pensioners, for instance, were allotted sixty days per year in the West) but the bureaucratic obstacles remained formidable and families were rarely allowed to travel together. As pressure to liberalize travel privileges increased, a law was passed in 1988 allowing family visits to the West for certain prescribed ceremonies, such as birthdays, weddings, anniversaries, and funerals. Until then, Bert only met his aunt on his home territory, which she invaded like a conquering queen.

Bert's aunt, accompanied by her youngest daughter, visited for the last time in 1988. Toward the end of the visit, Hildegard wrote in her diary: "I began singing as soon as I woke up this morning. I was ashamed as soon as I realized why. I was suddenly, in a single instant, happy—relieved, relaxed, and free. Because in five hours everything will be over." A week of hell was coming to a close.

"What I cannot stand," she wrote, "is how it is bound together with a forced toleration, with dishonesty, with silence about the economics of it all. I accept his relatives, but I don't love them, and I don't detect any love on their part. We tolerate each other. But worse, they pity us and think they're doing us a favor—they're doing us a favor!— by sacrificing themselves for us. I understand, and yet I don't understand, because the material exchange is no longer the only reason for it all, yet matters of the heart have had nothing to do with it for a long time."

Hildegard described the visit to me not long after she wrote this account. Bert's aunt, she felt, patronized her blatantly and almost brutally. Hildegard had planned "three days of culture" and three days of rest and sightseeing for the aunt's visit. She cleaned the apartment so "you could have looked into every corner," and she baked special foods hard to come by in the East.

"They came," Hildegard wrote, "with bread and cosmetics." The children, impressed by the fancy-looking cosmetics, incredulous that all that mascara could be meant as a gift, asked, "Are they going to take all that back with them?" Contemptuously, Hildegard took a tissue of rose-colored toilet paper (the guests had brought their own) and sniffed it delicately before blowing her nose in it. The children laughed. She sneered, "The new toilet paper, extra soft for the particularly sensitive ass!" The children howled.

Yet the children were entranced by the bearers of Western goods and so was Hildegard, in her unironic heart. When they exchanged gifts there were a bar of chocolate and automobile cards for the kids, a "cheap watch" for Hildegard.

"Everyone was happy but me," Hildegard wrote. "How could I say I was pleased with their cheap watch. If I said that I would be lying. Lying, lying, not to disappoint them."

The cheap watch was only the most overt insult. "They've gotten worse than ever. We speak only about things they want to talk about. I can't drink as much every evening as I drank on the first one [visit], just to force myself to be unconscious of the discussion. I'm tired of steadily complimenting them about their clothes. That's not so important to me."

What was important? Dignity. Hildegard was no longer a child—she stressed this to me—and she didn't need gifts or playthings. Yet the aunt constantly, irritatingly, asked her what she wanted from the great department store that was the Federal Republic. Hairspray? Brooches? Brushes? Perfumes, jewelry, nylons? Just say the word ... and Hildegard couldn't resist, even though it "wasn't important to her," even though she didn't really care. She allowed the aunt to direct her desires to things she inwardly condemned as tawdry. She took a childish pleasure in the promises of trinkets, and berated herself for it.

For years she had convinced herself that "used things from the West are still better than something new from here." What angered Hildegard so much was that though she no longer believed this to be true, she still behaved as if it were. "It was only partly true," she explained sheepishly, halfheartedly, "for if you had money you could look good here, too."

She took her in-laws to the theater, to a concert, to a ballet: "Not a single word of praise. They grumbled! The waiter was unfriendly, the coffee wasn't any good. No praise for my cooking and baking. No praise for my hairstyle, which I had changed for the first time in twenty years."

Then they wanted to go shopping. That enraged Hildegard because it gave them a chance to flaunt their wealth. Nothing was too expensive for them and nothing East Germany could produce was good enough. When they saw something of quality, they immediately dismissed it.

" 'We have that also at home, and that also, but ours is bigger, more beautiful, more colorful.' The crazy thing is that it's also probably true. Everything *is* better in the West"—Hildegard stops herself. "I don't need to discuss it further. But I want something else."

What else did she want? She had no idea. It was something inarticulable, ineffable, something hidden in the wells and recesses of fantasy.

Hildegard was quite right that the traffic between herself and her in-laws, her *need* for them despite her resentment, her lust for the cheap timepieces and gimcrack jewelry, had nothing to do with familial affection, but could not be reduced to simple material exchanges either. It wasn't the goods she wanted. She saw through the transparently delusive promise of the gift-wrapped gewgaws. They weren't better, prettier, pricier than East German saleables. They were shoddy wares. Yet she needed the promise itself, the idea that somewhere in the West there *were* better goods and more of them, cornucopias of cars and blue jeans and Swiss watches denied to her but enjoyed by her in-laws, utopias of white shoes with closed toes. She needed the fantasyland, the imaginary country of consumer goods, the absent object of desire. She resented her husband's relatives both for the imperious confidence with which they flaunted that dream country and their passports from it, and for the way their cheap gifts and accoutrements denied the dream. She resented her own experience, divided so cruelly between ordinary reality and the imagination's need.

The real traffic between Hildegard and her in-laws was one of images. The in-laws demanded and constructed for themselves an East of deprivation and want, to indulge their feelings of superiority. Hildegard desperately needed a supplementary West beyond the Wall in which her fantasies could find their proper home. It was a stringent, mutually reinforcing economy of desires, with Hildegard bound to come out the loser. The terms of the economy required her self-abasement. She had to keep an ingratiating face turned to the Westerners. It was precisely their superiority she resented—and required.

The evening before the guests' departure, Hildegard sang for them while Bert played the guitar. The next morning, the aunt's daughter complained that she couldn't sleep because one of the songs kept echoing in her ear.

"We had a real ear worm in our program," Hildegard wrote sarcastically in her diary, burning with anger at the insult. Yet she again lied to the aunt in a tearful good-bye, smoothing over hurt feelings while seething inside.

"It was really our pleasure," she said, "finally seeing you again."

Hildegard hopes that such one-sided visits are now over; finally she and Bert can visit the aunt. She doesn't know what will happen. She expects a great deal. Like moths drawn to the flame, Bert and Hildegard are planning two months of travel in West Germany during the summer of 1990.

7

Fear, Guilt, and Revenge

Hate must make a person productive,
otherwise one might as well love.
—Karl Kraus

FEAR, ENDURED AND TRANSFORMED

Fear—the German word is *Angst*—has always been a major technique for the control of peoples. This method of control reached new heights in the twentieth century as rulers began to employ new technologies of surveillance and punishment. Eastern European Stalinism, in its various forms in indigenous cultures, developed its own particular modes of control through fear. Labor camps of the Soviet type were not widely used in Eastern Europe. Rather, regimes played upon everyday fears to produce compliance and acquiescence, to bring about political quietude among the masses. The German cultural values of orderliness and discipline mixed well with this authoritarian control system, creating a particular version of rule by fear, with its own social contours and forms of individual psychology.

The collapse of the Wall not only signaled the end of the old regime, but also undermined other forms of East German local authority, which had hung its claim to obedience on the legitimacy of the political structure. With the opening of the border, most citizens, with a sudden rush of fearlessness, experienced this collapse of political authority as an immediate release from the particular apparatus of control by which they had been dominated. The release from fear, however, rarely resulted in a new-felt freedom. Rather, the fear turned to guilt and the guilt turned into a desire for revenge.

People who had acquiesced to the demands of the regime, who out of fear accepted routine humiliations rather than confront their masters, realized only after the opening of the Wall how they had been totally co-opted, remembering the countless times they had failed to stand up for ostracized colleagues, the numerous indignities suffered at the hands of minor functionaries, or even the privileges they had forgone out of anxiety over recriminations. Rather than feeling free, these people felt guilty, but not so guilty as they believed the perpetrators of the regime of fear should feel. The duped masses reserved their greatest anger for the leaders of the old regime, its ruling functionaries, and its Stasi protectors. Their anger, burdened by their own complicity, often turned to a desire for revenge.

The people who speak in this book—Regine, Hildegard, Helmut, Marina, Armin, and Franziska—had all lived with fear, and in many ways had acquiesced to its normalization and made peace with the regime. They had not been co-opted, however. "After the Wall" their fear did not result in a desire for revenge. In this chapter, I will explore what happened to them when the regime of fear broke down. How did they make their peace with their old adversaries? Why, when they seem to have every justification for wanting revenge, do they show such magnanimity?

FEAR AS A BEDFELLOW

Six weeks after the opening of the Wall I saw Hildegard and Bert at a birthday party for a mutual friend.

"Nothing has changed," Hildegard told me. "Absolutely nothing. Bert says the same thing." '

I asked her to be specific.

"Everything is different but nothing has changed," she replied with a kind of lighthearted seriousness.

They *seemed* different, Hildegard and Bert, this couple who for over 19 years had lived what she would describe as a "normal GDR life." They were more relaxed and optimistic than I had ever seen them. Yet something didn't seem right and at first I couldn't put my finger on it. It finally dawned on me: Hildegard was right. I had expected some dramatic change, a drastic difference, the visible mark of a revolution. Hildegard and Bert had been waiting for this brave new world for years, complaining bitterly to me in the past about the repressive order in the GDR. Now, with this order rapidly crumbling, I had looked for some profound, immediate shift in their behavior or in their sense of themselves. Instead, history seemed to have passed through their lives like a breeze through a well ordered room, ruffling a few papers but leaving no real trace.

It seemed very Western to me, this suburban imperturbability, this stolid, almost banal, backbone beneath ordinary life which stood up to all the transformations and catastrophes history might wreak. Only some time later, reflecting on what I knew of Hildegard, did I come to see it in a different light, as something deeper, more specific to the experience of citizens in an actually existing socialist country.

A couple of anecdotes will suffice to show what I mean. I first met Hildegard and Bert in September 1986, in the tiny one-room apartment of Frank, a composer. Hildegard was preparing for a career as a singer. A friend of mine had written the texts for her first musical program, Frank had written the music, and I was invited to come and listen to her practice. She wanted to quit work as a bookkeeper for the housing administration office and begin a musical career. That would be her third career, since she had taught school for six years before, as she described it, "I managed to escape the Ministry of Education."

Her work wasn't accounting in the sense I understand it. She didn't think it made much sense to keep strict books, given that between 30 and 70 percent of all the people who got apartments through her office did not pay rent. And, she added, there had been no inventory of properties for the last 11 years. The housing bureaucracy had no idea what they owned, and no incentive to find out. The discovery of more apartments would just mean more for them to administer. They much preferred doing nothing.

A week after our first meeting, Hildegard invited me to visit her at home. She and Bert seemed anxious to tell me a story.

The story was about the people who had occupied their apartment five years before, now resettled in the West. The husband had written a petition to leave. Such petitions took anywhere from six months to five years to get approved. The average time I heard mentioned by most people in 1986–88 was two years. The state discouraged applicants by long, inexplicable delays and bureaucratic hurdles. During the waiting period, petitioners were called in for repeated interviews to see if they still wanted to leave, with alternating strategies of harassment and enticement used to dissuade them.

After several years of waiting, the man took his case to the streets. He carried a banner down the sidewalk, proclaiming his desire to leave for the West. The police arrested him and the following day they seized his wife. The couple's three children were put in an orphanage, although the couple had relatives willing to take them in. The man was sentenced to five years' imprisonment, the woman to three years, for the crime of planning to flee the country, known as *Republikflucht*. In prison the wife went on a hunger strike to get her children released from the state-run orphanage and sent to relatives. The hunger strike was successful and later eventually the whole family was released to the West.

In hushed tones, Hildegard explained another "complication." Their present neighbors were also implicated in the matter, though no one really knew how. Shortly after the arrest of the former apartment dwellers, the police surrounded the entire building, finally forcing their way into the adjacent flat. They burst in with machine guns, as though they were raiding a terrorist stronghold. "Yes, John, with machine guns!"

The hapless family was arrested and made to lie face-down in the police van, to prevent them from seeing where they were going. But the couple kept resisting. Though handcuffed, they pushed themselves up to peer out the window, only to be forced down by blows on the back of their heads.

After an interrogation that lasted several days, they were released and went back to their apartment. The next day, they found both had been fired from their jobs. She had been a translator, he an engineer. She applied everywhere for work, but to no avail. Before this happened she was a lively, involved person, said Hildegard, but now she's a broken woman. With his background as an engineer, the man is handy at fixing things and finds odd jobs to support them. But both have now turned to the bottle. They've lost all their friends. The woman told Hildegard that she's too old to start over, so it doesn't make any sense for them to try to resettle in West Germany.

Hildegard and Bert seemed relieved to have told me this story. It mattered to them that I know this other side of life in the GDR. They also wanted me to know they were conscious of it, that it was a constant drumbeat at the back of their lives. They needed to put a different gloss on their own normality, to show how precarious their situation was despite its stable semblance and veneer.

Now, with the Wall fallen and the state in shards and rubble, I remembered something else about Hildegard's family. Their oldest son Konstantin once showed me two of his playthings, identity cards he had made for himself and his brother. He explained the details to me. On the right side of each card was an intricate code drawn from writing exercises used at his school. On the left side he included the details he supposed were on all identity cards:

Name: Kemper
First Name: Konstantin
Date of Birth: 2.6.78
Residence: John-Sieg-Str. 36
At the bottom of that side, he created his own category of belonging: Blood brother P2. This referred to the other identity card, on which he'd created a false identity as a spy:
Cover Name: Konstantin Libonsky
Date of Birth 2.6.78
Residence: Kaskelstrasse 24
Telephone: at your pleasure #97350168
For his spy self, Konstantin changed his family name and residence, and invented a coveted telephone number (his family had been on a waiting list for eight years). He explained that he used "blood brother" because that was how the Indians used to identify people they trusted.

GDR law required adults to carry an identity card at all times. Only juveniles were exempt. GDR citizens often asked me if it were true that in America one was not required to carry an identity card. The need to identify oneself at all times to a ubiquitous and intrusive state was inescapable. The mechanism of social control insinuated itself into the playtime fantasies of Hildegard's children. Even wild Indians had to have mock government licenses.

Now, retrospectively, I contemplated the degree to which domination had become domesticated in the GDR, the extent to which fear had become integrated into the habits and practices, the dream spaces and ludic intervals, of everyday life. Was it reasonable to expect drastic changes in people's ordinary experiences when those ordinary experiences had, for so long, been shaped by a process of accepting and of coming to terms with fear?

"WE ARE EVERYWHERE"

When army general Erich Mielke, head of the state security (Stasi) since 1957, was called to testify before the East German parliament on 13 November 1989, he defended the Orwellian apparatus he had built by proclaiming, "I love, but I love you all!" Before his tearful eyes, a whole history switched gears from tragedy to farce. Forty years of beatings became a retrospective embrace.

No East German could be comforted by Mielke's *confessio amantis*. The Stasi's love was that of a sadistic Peeping Tom. The internal slogan of the state security— "We are everywhere"—was one of the few statements of the duplicitous East German state that could be taken at face value. Every post office had its room for intercepting mail, nearly all phones were wiretapped, and millions of apartments were bugged. Virtually every public or private assembly of any sort (Jehovah's Witness meetings, university seminars, gay bars, gardening clubs) had a Stasi agent in attendance to report on what was said and often to provoke comment that was later denounced. Wherever two or three were gathered in anybody's name, there was the Stasi also. Just before its dissolution, the Stasi employed 85,000 full-time workers and 109,000 "unofficial workers." They had a huge stock of rifles, panzers, hand grenades, and machine guns; owned 2,037 buildings, apartments, and country houses, with 652 in East Berlin alone; had 24 vacation spas with 2,058 beds as well as exclusive hospitals and sport facilities for Stasi workers only; and had a yearly budget of 3.6 billion marks ($2 billion calculated at its internal GDR value). The central Stasi headquarters in Berlin-Lichtenberg, just around the corner from Hildegard's apartment, encompassed 3,000 rooms.

The law of 8 February 1950 that created the state security did not specify its tasks or size and put no limit on the domains of its authority. Officially the state security was to "prevent surprises from the *Gegner* (adversary/opponent)," and "prevent subversion." Egon Krenz, who later was put in charge of security for the ruling party, described the Stasi as "a state within a state." Citizen committees later investigating the Stasi found internal documents stating that three fundamental rules governed its activities:

1. Every person is a potential security risk
2. One must know everything in order to be secure
3. Security takes precedence over the law.

At the heart of Stasi operations was Division XX, responsible for dissidents. The *Gegner* within was always the obsessive object of the Stasi's twisted love. Internal dissent ebbed as the Stasi extended its sway. By the early 1980s, the state appeared to have eliminated most of its adversaries either by shipping them to West Germany or by silencing them. The next few years, however, saw a revival of opposition activities. Ecological and human rights groups, especially within the churches, were focal points of dissent.

The SED regime became increasingly paranoid about the general negative mood in the country. Its fears were reflected in a tightening of internal security within the Stasi itself. Increased militarization of the entire apparatus was accompanied by war games lasting three to four days. Stasi agents were trained to fight to the death in the event of a revolt or a Western invasion, while their children would be evacuated to the Soviet Union. In this game, with the enemy standing at the door in West Berlin, agents had only a few hours to round up their wives and children. The entire game was played with deadly seriousness, as if the crisis were real, causing considerable anxiety among the agents and their families who were forbidden to talk about its ramifications.

Stasi workers were trained to mistrust each other. Agent spied on agent in a massive spy network. Forced to give up all contact with family and friends not part of the apparatus, they were encouraged to spend their free time with other Stasi agents and their families. Special privileges were ladled out to keep the agents happy within their highly controlled and regulated world. These privileges—Czech cars (Ladas), better food, higher pay, bigger apartments or homes, access to higher education for their children— became a source of instant, open resentment after the opening of the Wall.

WITH FREEDOM A GROWING FEAR

Regine—the good socialist Regine—can stand as a paradigmatic story of a different sort. Never a *Mitläufer*, someone who just went along, she had always maintained her integrity and independence. Hence for Regine, fear did not turn into guilt after the fall of the Wall. And revenge could not have been further from her mind.

She was called in by the Stasi three times. The first time was in 1961 when a former lover of hers was arrested for "inflammatory remarks against the state."

"In stores and bars, he would get very loud and complain, 'This damned cheese here is no good,' or 'There are only shortages here,' or some such thing. He served two years for that."

She found a lawyer to defend him, causing the Stasi to suspect her of being an accomplice. "The Stasi asked me what I knew about him, and I told them. I always treated the Stasi respectfully, because they were more imprisoned than I was. I felt sorry for them having to administer these ridiculous inquisitions."

Regine was summoned by the Stasi a second time in 1971, again on a matter concerning her former lover. After his release from prison, he had married, had two children (aged five and six in 1971) and begun working as a journalist. He wrote an article critical of the state, published (under a pseudonym) by the West German weekly *Die Zeit*.

Regine was questioned for seven hours. "I was honest, but I would never have said anything to incriminate him. They knew that and even asked me if I would. I said no, of course not. But I would address them in ways that forced them to respect me. I would say things like, 'As intelligent people, we can agree,' or 'Just between us.' They made me sign a protocol of what I had said. I insisted they rewrite it several times so it reflected exactly my intention, which irritated them, but they did it. His wife was also arrested. She was sentenced to three years in prison; he to seven. I helped look after the children for the next couple of years, before they were released and bought by the West Germans." (The West Germans regularly ransomed political prisoners.)

Regine had a run-in with the Stasi in 1979 when Rudolf Bahro, the author of *Die Alternative*, was released from prison. Bahro had written most of his celebrated critique of "actually existing socialism" at Regine's dining room table. Shortly before completing it, he removed it from her apartment to avoid incriminating her if the police came. After its publication in West Germany in 1977, he was arrested and given a seven years' sentence for treason.

"I experienced the most primal fear of my life," Regine remembers, "when I heard he was arrested. It was sheer helplessness. Everybody was talking about the book. I had told Wolfgang Harich, the philosopher, about the fascinating book that Bahro was writing."

Harich had been imprisoned for high treason after a well publicized show trial in 1957. At that trial, he incriminated himself and admitted to the absurd charge of plotting with a group of West Berlin agents to overthrow the Ulbricht regime. Within the same year Harich became the star witness for the state prosecutor in another show trial, that of Walter Janka, former resistance fighter and at that time the chief of Aufbau Publishing House.

When Harich learned of Bahro's arrest, he called Regine and urged her to go to the Stasi and tell them everything she knew. Since he knew where Bahro had written the book, he might also be implicated at the trial. His health wasn't good enough to live through another imprisonment, he told her. It would be best if she revealed everything on her own. Regine replied, "I might someday jump off the television tower on Alexander Platz, but I would never go to them and denounce myself for something where I had done no wrong. Never would I sink to that humiliation."

Bahro was released after serving two years of his sentence. He was given two weeks to gather his things together and leave for West Germany.

"Police thought he'd come to me," said Regine, "so they watched my apartment, with men before my door day and night and on the roof and in the basement. This produced very different reactions in people. Some whom I hardly knew went out of their way to greet me when they saw me; others whom I knew well avoided me altogether. Only once did they ask me for my identification, and that was all."

In 1980, Regine was called in by the Stasi a third time after an African friend who had stayed with her telephoned from her apartment to arrange the flight of a GDR citizen to West Berlin. This time she sat for four hours at Stasi headquarters. "They cited my own sentences back to me. But I always answered their questions truthfully. I had nothing to hide."

Regine's reaction is curious. She remembers the old GDR as an atmosphere of fear, yet it seems curiously rational to her, stable and predictable in its intimidation, an atmosphere in which her professions were met, if not with respect, at least with attention. One feels she almost perversely enjoyed the interrogations as places wherein her private voice, cultivated in quiet interactions, took on a certain public authority.

It's an idiosyncratic response, rooted in Regine's own individual romance of socialism, in the lucky invulnerability of her world of private images and values. It also reflects the degree to which the intimidation the state imposed was orderly, manageable. It could be circumvented by a Jesuitical attention to the rules; it could be domesticated.

Fear became a defined and ordered aspect of the East German's everyday experience. It was expected. For many East Germans, the removal of the apparatus of fear brought feelings of guilt at having gone along and a desire for revenge against the perpetrators who had duped them so easily so long.

Regine, on the other hand, felt little anger, for she had never internalized the fear. Disorder is what Regine fears: the unexpectable and unaccountable, rupturing the regularized and known. The potential chaos of mass anger unsettles her.

"I fear the reaction of the masses, that's my great concern. Because I know how that goes in Germany. I know through my work as a documentarist for films. Those images [from the 1930s] are always before my eyes, and my fear grows every time I see pictures of the German masses." The upwelling of public resentment and rage that followed the years of terror thus seems to her particularly terrifying. Within weeks of the opening of the Wall, Regine had an experience that sent her into a panic. On the train from Leipzig to Berlin she was the personal target of what she called a neo-Fascist threat, a threat she saw sweeping the land. She was talking with two strangers about the long-term impact of the collapse of the regime, when a middle-aged man—Regine thought him a working-class or lower-level functionary—sitting across the aisle began ranting about the damage done by foreigners working in the German economy, especially Poles and Vietnamese, and about the responsibility of intellectuals for the current crisis. He punctuated his comments with references to "the damned pigs." She finally went up to the man, to have, in her direct way, an *Auseinandersetzung*, a confrontation, with him.

"Quit this nonsense. Who do you think you are, saying those things?" argued Regine. "It isn't the foreigners you should hate. They aren't causing our problems."

"You intellectual *Ziege*, goat!" he screamed back, red in the face, taking another slug of beer. "You deserve *eine in die Fresse*, a good punch in the nose!"

Chastened but undaunted, Regine continued to reason with him. She tried to explain the situation of the foreign workers in East Germany, now totaling over 50,000. The man kept drinking, now and then mumbling, "*Halt die Fresse oder du kriegst eine*, shut your mouth or you'll get it." Even after she returned to her seat, convinced at last he really might hit her, he kept grumbling about the she-goat who dared to challenge him.

The sheltered intellectual meeting the angry man ...

The encounter haunted Regine. The man's anger seemed unprecedented, unaccountable. She groped for a context for his behavior, finding it in the growing right-wing—she would say neo-Fascist—movements in both Germanies. The West German *Republikaner* party, a far right political party that uses the vocabulary and slogans of the Third Reich, had in early 1989 garnered 7.5 percent of the vote in elections in Berlin and Frankfurt.

"If fascism comes," she explained to me, still thinking of the man on the train, "I'll be one of the first to have to go. Anti-Communist, anti-Semite, anti-intellectual. Those were the characteristics of German fascism in the 1930s. I lived through that as a child. I know how it begins. And now I feel more threatened than any time since my childhood."

Regine is not alone in feeling threatened. So do the other members of a group of GDR women writers who meet regularly to share their work.

"This last time we met in my apartment here in Prenzlauer Berg. Before, we were united in our opposition to Stalinism, to the regime, to the arms race, to poverty and exploitation in the Third World. But this time when we met it was different. Everyone arrived on time, and as they came in we were all nearly in tears. We all hugged each other out of joy and relief at having each other. Before we were all against something. We shared a simple opinion against Stalinism.

"Now we sensed something different, and what we sensed was a movement in the same direction. A fear. Suddenly we were talking about emigrating, or perhaps establishing a colony with Christa [Wolf], for she lives on a large chunk of land in the country."

I asked how her work unit was treating its Stasi people

(every work unit in the country had at least one Stasi agent assigned to it).

"We had them, too. And in a meeting in early December we voted never again to work with several of them. One of them was allowed to work further with us as a film director, but he was no longer allowed to be head of a section of the studio. Even our *Kaderleiter* [the SED leader in the work unit] was in favor of getting rid of them. They're now getting unpaid vacation.

"I'll also oppose them in the future. They were international Stalinists. They broke the will of so many valuable people; they damaged so many souls."

Yet she hesitates . . . the man on the train. . . . "Look," she said to me, "I am also a victim of this revolution. This corruption stuff really doesn't concern me. I was by far happier under the state before, when the Stasi used to stand outside my door—that bothered me far less."

UNIVERSAL REVENGE

Regine is not unique in fearing a people newly freed from fear. Helmut expressed many of the same anxieties to me.

"The reason the Autumn Revolution was free of violence," he maintained, "was not because reason ruled the streets, but because people had *Angst*." They were trained to be passive, submissive, and were only beginning to lose their ingrained habits.

"And the reason why there is increasing violence here now is that the people have no more fear." This removal of fear accompanying the collapse of the regime has resulted in an increase in crime and a general defiance of all forms of public authority.

"In capitalism," Helmut contends, "people are regulated by the market, and the market is most interested in efficiency. In socialism, it is fear of losing one's position that regulates people. This fear is maintained through a system of orders from above.

"Once the regime collapsed in November, people began losing respect for the authorities here, for the entire set of administrators who had ruled them through fear and repression. But we do not yet have the efficiency-structure characteristic of capitalism. People here have not been disciplined to respect legitimate rule by the powerful; they obey authority out of fear only.

"Now the fear has been replaced by revenge, a need for revenge, because people are ashamed of their fear, of how they cooperated with the regime. And that was repressed for so long. But now, it's as if they have a knife digging into their heads forcing them to strike out. They are aggressive as well as feeling themselves to be victims. Those of us who had not been co-opted do not feel ourselves victims of the regime, nor do we seek revenge, largely because we were never so completely motivated by fear."

The crumbling of the GDR's power structure was accompanied by an orgy of recriminations and reprisals. Stasi agents and collaborators were ferreted out everywhere. Because the Stasi tended to live in apartment complexes especially built for them, many of the agents were easily identified. In small towns, they could readily be hunted down by their former victims, often their neighbors. North of Berlin, for example, a citizen action group reappropriated a former housing settlement for the elderly in the middle of a wooded area that had been taken over and made into a modern Stasi compound. Local citizens forced the mayor to reopen to the public the park around the settlement, to return half of the homes to the elderly and rent the other half to private citizens. (In other districts, however, such as Berlin-Pankow, quick-thinking local party officials and Stasi agents worked together on the district council to purchase legally for token sums the villas they had expropriated from wealthy citizens who had either fled or been released to the West.)

The reprisals were hardly limited to reclaiming property, however. Between December 1989 and the March 1990 election, citizen committees responsible for investigating and disbanding the Stasi often found themselves in the role not only of sealing Stasi offices so documents could not be destroyed, but also of protecting ex-agents from the vengeance of angry crowds.

A committee called "Women for Change" in the city of Erfurt began the popular action against the Stasi at noon on 4 December 1989. After failing to mobilize their mayor and the prosecutor's office, they occupied the local Stasi buildings and forced the sealing of all rooms where documents and dossiers could be found, using the authority of a nearby military prosecuting lawyer. Word of this action spread rapidly throughout the republic and within hours similar actions took place in other cities. Soon citizen committees had forced access into all fourteen regional Stasi headquarters.

In a climate of residual fear, suspicion and second-guessing were ubiquitous. The salvaged files revealed that a substantial percentage of the population were collaborators. The first wave of retribution had focused on the readily identifiable Stasi agents in their villas and compounds. A second wave now turned on the real or imaginary enemy within, a paranoiac move that echoed the obsessive self-inquisitions staged by the Stasi itself.

Anyone might be an ex-informant. Many suspect these "stormings" were in fact organized by the Stasi to legitimate the stealing and destruction of documents (which occurred on a massive scale) and to create sympathy for the Stasi as victims of citizen hysteria.

A member of the Erfurt committee later set up to investigate the Stasi estimated that up to one-third of the committee members were probably either former Stasi agents or sent by the Stasi. The investigators had no way of knowing for sure.

The interim Modrow regime, which initially resisted the total dismemberment of the security apparatus, eventually assigned the task of disbanding the Stasi to a three-member committee. By February it appeared that all state security activity had been stopped and by April the committee took on the role of investigating members of the newly elected parliament for past collaboration with the Stasi.

One of the major questions that remains is the fate of former Stasi agents. Agents and informers still are, as individuals, everywhere. The parallels to denazification following World War II are striking. Opinion is divided as to whether to grant an amnesty, as the West Germans did to the Nazis in 1951, or to prosecute former agents for specific crimes, as the East Germans did in their denazification process.

Most former Stasi workers are in precarious employment situations. In most industries, people refuse to work with them. "No Stasi Need Apply" signs accompany many job postings. In March, I was startled to see a "help wanted" sign outside a theater in East Berlin carrying the added message "Former Stasi Also Welcome." A friend, equally surprised, could only suggest that theater people must be more tolerant.

In addition to tales of paper pushers and bureaucratic functionaries punished after the revolution, there are stories of mighty figures fallen low. These often have a particular pathos. Few leaders of the old regime escaped entirely unscathed and some were singled out for particular vengeance.

In the early days of the revolution, revenge was directed against Alexander Schalck-Golodkowski, responsible for official smuggling operations for the ostensible purposes of obtaining Western currency and Western technology. Schalck fled to West Berlin as soon as it became apparent the regime would fall. He was arrested by West Berlin police in December and sent to the Berlin-Moabit prison. In mid-January, Western authorities released him against the wishes of the citizen committees and the citizen's round table in East Berlin. During his prison stay, he had met repeatedly with officials of the West German Office of Constitutional Protection, regaling them with details of his illegal dealings with Western European politicians. In the end, it seemed more prudent to let him off lightly.

With Schalck out of sight, protected by the West German police, vengeance was directed toward the former All-Highest of the German Democratic Republic, the recent head of party and state, Erich Honecker. Honecker's life may eventually be seen as a signal tragedy of this century, Shakespearian in its outlines, Brechtian in its crude and cruel irony.

At the age of fourteen, Honecker bravely broke off all relations with the Lutheran religion in which he had been raised and became a believing Communist. In 1935, convicted of plotting treason, he was sentenced to 10 years in prison by the Nazis. He was initially charged with the same crime in East Germany after the revolution.

Honecker, once an inmate of KZ Brandenburg, became the leader of a rump but still real state. In 1989, 63 years after his initial arrest in the Third Reich, he was a virtual exile in his shattered country, expelled from the Socialist Unity party, denied protection by the state. Released from the Charité Hospital on 29 January 1990, after recovering from severe abdominal disorders Honecker was immediately arrested and taken to the prison in Berlin-Rummelsburg. After his release from prison (and pending a decision whether to try him), the only home he could find was with the Lutheran church, the very church he had rejected and treated as an enemy.

Pastor Uwe Holmer of the small village of Lobetal, agreed to give Honecker and his wife Margot a room in his own home. The Honeckers had no choice. Everywhere else they were hounded by enraged mobs. The aged couple engaged in all the rituals of the pastor's house, including premeal prayer. The minister, known as a radical pietist, cited the Bible in defense of his decision: "Love your enemy as your friend." Holmer's family had been politically persecuted by the communists, suffering particularly from the policies of Margot Honecker as Minister of Education. Not one of his ten children was allowed to attend the advanced high school, though all had adequate grades. He regarded caring for the Honeckers as a "mission of God."

In the first months of their stay, Holmer received hundreds of letters from citizens, nearly all crying for revenge instead of mercy. Some believers even announced they were leaving the church. Holmer persisted in his charity. In March, shortly before the election, state officials arranged for an apartment for the Honeckers, but within hours of their arrival, residents in the apartment block began threatening the new guests and officials were obliged to take the Honeckers back to the pastor in Lobetal. Honecker is in poor health and is reported to be emotionally withdrawn. He and his wife both refuse to accept any blame for the catastrophes of 1989 or for the 40 years of fear preceding them.

A RESIDUE OF FEAR

Hildegard began working in a new cabaret in the summer of 1989. With three actors and a piano player, she performed twice a month. As the political events unfolded that autumn, the group constantly rewrote the scripts.

"Our goal was and still is to encourage the people to stay here, to encourage them to be positive about themselves." When I saw the cabaret act in September, before the collapse of the regime, they were aiming small jabs at politicians without naming them. By November, they were doing caricatures of Honecker and Krenz.

Hildegard's heart isn't in the satire, however. For herself and her husband, politics was always an intrusion. "I'm not a political person," Hildegard explained. "Those are people who do important things, people who are willing to stick their necks out in public life. I'm an artist. I hope that I do something worthwhile and valuable through my art, through the cabaret I'm engaged in. You know, these events have sort of trapped me. I haven't been active in the demonstrations, but really, Stefan Hermlin [an old communist writer, and a hero of the resistance during the Second World War] doesn't go to demonstrations either."

Under the GDR regime, Hildegard adjusted herself resignedly to the fear, to the restrictions placed on public space and public expression and she has managed the transition to a more open society well. The temptation to turn liberation into general rancor, to settle old scores, never gnawed at her. She never succumbed to the frenzy of revenge. Yet the nagging sense of some responsibility overlooked, some opportunity missed, remains. She excuses herself over and over.

"I've been only to the large demo on 4 December here in Berlin. I have my children to think of. The critical attitudes Bert and I have about politics have never helped them. They never got good grades in civics. For example, Bert has recently been saying, 'Those damn pigs,' about the politicians, but the children understand that differently [more as humor than defamy] and repeat it in the school, thinking Bert means something broader."

We sit in her apartment in Berlin-Lichtenberg on John-Sieg-Strasse, named after yet another resistance fighter, and she returns fixedly to the subject.

"Taking part in the demos, no, that would have been an exceptional decision," she insists. "I had to think of the others. Back then, in October, I still had to think of my children before I did something like go to a demonstration. Look at that apartment building over there." She points out the window. Across the street were other *Neubau* like the one we were in, a row of ten-story apartment complexes with stark facades, indistinguishable from one another. "Those apartments are all filled with Stasi people. You can see that in the kinds of cars they drive and how they handle themselves in the grocery store."

I think about the legacy of fear that still persists, in the constriction, the wizening, of space for public discourse under the old regime, the introjected habit of self-checking, self-silencing, that will not quite die.

Perhaps Regine managed best over the years of uncertainty, rooted in her completely private realm of references, inaccessible to the Stasi and their inquisitions. The public life and the communal voice of East Germany, however, will take a long time to recover from the atomization and the strangling.

"We feared another China Solution here, and you know, it nearly came to that. I knew if I went out on the street that was it, I could be arrested, and then not only I but my whole family would have to pay."

8

Becoming Capitalist

No one is more a slave than he who thinks he is free without being so.

—Goethe, *Elective Affinities*

A HEAVY COST

Since the Autumn Revolution, East Germany has begun reconstructing itself on a capitalist model. Culture, state, and economy will all be revamped radically. Over time, the whole integument of life in East German territory will be cast off and replaced. This conversion is taking place in a peculiarly German way, from the top down. The emerging capitalist society, much like the socialism that preceded it, is being planned. The advisors come not from Moscow but from Bonn. They are not apparatchiks but businessmen and bankers. The shape of the capitalist transformation will be decided in complicated negotiations in closed rooms between the powerful West Germans and the enervated East Germans.

Long after the Wall fell, the primary issue in most East Germans' minds was whether the 176 billion East marks in private hands would be exchanged at a one-to-one rate for deutschmarks. Once the West German government announced the generous exchange terms that would accompany currency reform in July 1990, a huge if transient spasm of relief swept over the East. No one could imagine for long, however, that the problems East Germany faced were as simple as trading in worthless currency. Greater and more demanding difficulties lay ahead.

As of April 1990 the GDR already had a foreign debt of 34 billion deutschmarks, as well as a domestic debt of 160 billion East marks. Both are likely to skyrocket once plant closings begin in the fall of 1990. Unification means that the Federal Government must assume this debt, leaving less money available for drastically needed investment. The repair of the crumbling infrastructure (especially streets and railways), installation of a modern telephone system, and environmental cleanups will create an enormous drain on Western resources. Huge sums are involved. Over 200 billion deutschmarks are needed to modernize the transportation system and another 750 billion deutschmarks for apartment maintenance and renovation. The East has only 20 billion to offer.

Correcting ravages committed against nature, the legacy of decades of intensive industrialization unchecked by any environmental policies, is perhaps the heaviest burden East Germans have to bear. East Germany, according to the

West Berlin-based German Institute for Economic Research, is 10 years behind Western environmental standards. Each year East German environmental damages amount to an additional 30 billion deutschmarks. Dying or dead lakes number at least 9,000; two-thirds of the groundwater is "somewhat or strongly polluted"; and GDR air pollution is ten times worse than in the Federal Republic.

To clean up the poisoned rivers and lakes alone will cost around 100 billion deutschmarks. Hefty expenditures such as this will almost certainly paralyze the fledgling capitalist economy. As a further obstacle, the cleanup must be accompanied by tougher environmental laws. Such standards will force more plant closures, increasing unemployment.

Because of the abruptness of the transformation to capitalism, because they are being colonized so swiftly by their neighbor state to the West, East Germans face more sudden dislocations than do their fellow Eastern Europeans. Overnight the structures and guarantees that offered them safety are being whisked away. Overnight they must reorder their entire lives. *Kapital* alone counts now, where myriad complicated arrangements and compromises once ruled.

Over four decades, the GDR, anxious to prove its self-sufficiency to the West, built up and subsidized a multitude of industries, producing their own "cheaper" shoes, cars, radios, and televisions. These industries gave the appearance of competitiveness, but in reality consistently lost money. With the protected market for their goods gone, they will for the most part go bankrupt. Indeed, East German productive capacity is at an advanced stage of collapse. Over half of all GDR companies in May 1990 were producing at a loss, with only 32 percent turning a profit.

Unemployment is thus the one certain feature on the

horizon of East Germany's future. Estimates of joblessness range from 1 million (projected by the German Institute for Economic Research) to 3.5 million (estimated by Dresden economist Albert Jugel), the latter representing over one-third of a working population of 8.6 million. Women comprise 50 percent of the work force in the GDR. They will undoubtedly bear disproportionate costs in the transition to capitalist production. The workers hardest hit by closures, the first to lose their jobs, are single mothers, who make up 34 percent of all GDR mothers (and 48 percent of mothers in East Berlin).

It should be apparent why economically flourishing West German firms are not investing in the GDR as many East Germans at first expected them to do. Such firms can easily produce enough goods to feed GDR demands without expanding their present productive capacity or investing in aged, outmoded East German plants or machinery. It is more profitable, at least in the short run, to view the Easterners in terms of their consumption capacity rather than their productive one. Hence, while demand for Western goods increases in the East, it stimulates production in the West, not investment in the East, a pattern typical of Third World "development projects."

If this situation changes, it will only be because the buying power of East German citizens seems likely to drop drastically. After the currency reforms taking effect on 1 July 1990, East Germans will be buying products at international market prices. Their subsidies on rents and foodstuffs will for the most part be eliminated. Meantime, East German wages are (and are likely to remain) approximately one-third of the West German average. East German women earn only 60 percent of what men earn.

Current differences in East and West German productivity rates tell a miserable story. A West German works 3 minutes for a bottle of beer, an East German works 7; for a stick of butter, a West German works 7 minutes, an East German 1 hour and 27 minutes; for a color television an East German works 9 times as long; for a washing machine 7 times as long. Such disparities may take more than a decade to overcome.

The capitalism being imported into the GDR will only slowly, with struggle and sacrifice, raise the standard of living of East Germans. Moreover, East Germans add to their own problems by indulging in short-term thinking, rather than contemplating the long-term effects of their consumption patterns, a failing perhaps understandable when the long-term prospects are numinous and subject to daily change, but nonetheless dangerous and self-destructive. The mass East German buying spree in West Berlin that began with the opening of the Wall has led to a huge drain of financial resources out of the country. It has also resulted in vast and chronic surpluses of East German goods. No one will buy them.

How will East Germans adapt to their uncertain new world? The most radical changes will no doubt come in subtler regions, less accessible to statistical analysis, in the behaviors and practices, the norms and values, of the East Germans, as they reconstruct themselves in compliance with the new system.

What changes will be required? What habits left over from the socialist regime will be conserved and what kinds of self-conceptions and actions will disappear into the dustbin of history? The question of how a socialist training, a socialist identity, can be transformed into a capacity for effective action in a capitalist society is already a subject of intense importance to the East Germans. Their reflections on the changes awaiting them, their meditations on their shifting experiences, offer insights into the relationship— far from completely oppositional—between the two long-opposed systems.

PLUS ÇA CHANGE . . .

The events in autumn 1989 did not catch Helmut and Marina by surprise. Helmut had sensed a sourness in the country's mood when I met with him that summer. It was "stink sour," he said, and even the promise of collective rest and relaxation as most East Germans headed for some sun in the Balkans couldn't ease the tension. He expected something to give. "It can't go on like this," he said, "the pressure is mounting."

Already a kind of creeping conquest was taking place. Price tags were quietly being hung on the entire nation.

"Our regime has been selling us out for years. This summer I saw a village where they are selling the cobblestone streets, the original ones from the Middle Ages, to West Germany. Can you believe it? They're selling our streets! And where is the money going? All the best things we produce are being exported."

His sense of the tension was characteristically rooted in a conception of East Germany as inadequate, as left behind. He spoke as though freedom were a fashion trend, and the frumpy GDR was wearing last year's style.

"We feel like we're the last asses again," he said, "with something happening in Poland and Hungary. And nothing here yet. Nothing! We paid reparations for World War II— the West Germans didn't—and it's *our* standard of living that declines. The West Germans are getting wealthier!

Now they come to Budapest and Prague, and we can't even get into restaurants. The people don't want to serve us unless we have foreign currency.

"We can't buy the products which we ourselves produce. I don't care about imported goods, I'm talking about our own products, like furniture and textiles. Even the Czechs are getting wealthier, and I thought we were always doing better than they. Now our regime wants to close the door on access to Czechoslovakia, the only country in the world where we can go without a visa. I've heard they're starting to make plans for us next year to be able to travel to Albania. They can fly us in and fly us out, the people there are locked in also. There you have it: East Germany—Albania—Rumania. A triad of true socialists."

The fall of the Wall, the end of the long imprisonment, didn't alleviate Helmut's sense of entrapment. It exacerbated it. He felt a comprehensive and terrifying loss of control over the circumstances of his life. Virtually every certainty in the East Germans' world, from the political structure that laid down the outlines of the citizens' lives to the most elemental aspects of existence—prices, rents, and job security, dissolved into air.

It is a commonplace that capitalism speeds up the experience of time for its subjects. As one writer brilliantly put it, in the late eighteenth century, under conditions of capitalist production, "there began an extraordinary and exponential multiplication of the objects available for contemplation. The things that could be known increased; so . . . did the means of recording and transmitting them, until the circulation of facts embarked on an incessant acceleration to ever more incredible speeds."[1]

For the inhabitants of East Germany it was as though the gears shifted from first to fourth, or fortieth, in a few seconds. The successive accelerations Westerners had undergone in the decades since the end of World War II were all foisted on Easterners at once. The repressive predictability of socialist experience was replaced by a continual, almost daily, onslaught of change.

Helmut and Marina found that they could make no solid plans amid the flux. At first Helmut had hoped to start, with some friends, a journal to be called *Flipper*, in the eccentric tradition in West Germany of Left journals with maritime names. It was virtually impossible to compete, however, with the welter of West German-initiated and -financed projects. Meantime there were other uncertainties to confront, problems and doubts that stole away the precious time necessary to carry anything to fulfillment. Rents in the GDR, which averaged 5 percent of wages, were expected to increase to at least five times that. Helmut and Marina risked losing their apartment. They at least owned some solid property of a sort. During the summer, Marina and Helmut spent much of their time in a country house Marina inherited from her family, but the circumstances of reunification place that inheritance in doubt.

In the early days of land reform during the Russian occupation, people voted in a series of referendums to expropriate land from the conservative Junker class. Marina's parents obtained their country house through such an expropriation, from a local count who had moved to West Germany. It became their "personal" property. As GDR law did not recognize private property, Marina's parents could pass the house on to their children but could not give or sell it to anyone else, including relatives or friends. Marina had, however, the security of a lifelong lien on it.

With impending reunification many former Junker families are returning to the GDR to reclaim their land. The

West German Basic Law, in some legal opinion, recognizes expropriations performed by referendum (as opposed to those by fiat), but the ultimate legal status of the property following annexation remains in doubt.

Employment presented still other problems. Since Helmut is a pediatrician, his earning power seemed relatively secure but he was already experiencing jealousy and anger that he was earning less than his western counterparts.

"After all," he complained, "they work fewer hours with more modern equipment, but earn four to five times more money."

Marina, meanwhile, might well lose her job with Henschel Publishing House, which publishes all drama in the GDR. She was finding her working situation increasingly tense. She had remained a party member until just before the March elections.

"Somebody must stay in to help clean things up," she told me. "We can't leave the party to the old Stalinists. It's still the most powerful political organization in this country. But what sort of hell my coworkers at the publishing house have put me through! As if I was responsible for this mess! The others want only to talk about all the corruption, shit, and dirt in the party. The boss's secretary said to me in late December, 'Aren't you ashamed of yourself?' And people sneer at me nearly daily. 'Are you still in the party today?' I've even heard of party members in other cities getting lynched. The slogan goes: 'Each must shoot a Russ[ian].'

"Here I am, on the wrong side again, with the office workers and intellectuals angry at me. Just last week, someone at work said to me: 'That word "party"—I can't bear to hear it any more.' "

For Marina, the revulsion against the party is not so

much a reasoned response as a mass scapegoating. In the new atmosphere of rapid-fire instability, people seize on any explanation or assignment of blame that allows them to give a momentary order and intelligibility to their experience. Clichés abound amid the wreck.

Karin identifies herself with the reformed Communist party and speaks in a collective voice: "We really have no time to think about what to do. The people fear we are going to conduct experiments on them again. It's much safer just to turn their lives over to the Federal Republic. The saying goes: rather an end with horror than horror without end."

Helmut concurs. Underneath all the glitter and glitz of speed and sleekness, underneath the chrome-plated veneer of incessant change, lurks a malignant regularity, he argues. The chaos serves the purposes of a surreptitious order. No less than the old socialist regime, the new capitalist system preys on people's fears. It reduces the citizenry to passivity and incomprehension no less effectively than did the old, repressive order. Only the objects of apprehension and awe have changed. People no longer fear the iron fist, but the fetishized commodity. The sick feeling of inadequacy among the populace in the pit of the its stomach remains the same.

Marina likes to tell the story of her former brother-in-law, an ex-Stasi agent, who went to the West immediately after the Wall came down. He returns often to visit. Marina noted that after four weeks on the job in a small company, he still didn't know what he was producing and, as a low-level worker, he was using more primitive technology than he was familiar with here.

"In socialism, we place so much emphasis on technology and on knowing what the whole product is, even when one only produces a part of it. There, he was never informed what he was making." The former apparatchik became part of a real machine, an incognizant cog in a genuinely indifferent apparatus.

As intellectuals, Helmut and Marina perhaps naturally see the spectacle of individual East Germans' confusion and alienation most poignantly summed up in the loss of the ability to express onself. The GDR and its citizens, they feel, have lost their voices. Colonized by alien words, their own meanings expropriated, the people can only ventriloquize an increasingly foreign language of prices, slogans, clichés. The price tags Helmut saw insidiously settling over the East German landscape were the harbingers of a general, authoritative resignification. Everything is now labeled and up for sale and the people have little voice in, can barely mouth a protest against, the revaluation.

Not that the old regime furnished a freer space for self-expression. But Helmut remembers one moment. . . . It was at the 4 November demonstration on Alexander Platz. There, surrounded by a forest of banners, of homemade signs and statements, amid a chorus of conflicting voices still somehow unanimous in their excitement, Helmut for the first time in his life as a GDR citizen experienced a sense of social solidarity.

"That was both the beginning and end of socialism," he recalls, "the first time I ever felt proud to be a citizen of the GDR. Then it was all over. The rage directed against the Party suddenly was transformed into rage against socialism.

"On 16 October, I still remember that everything was open, it could have turned out otherwise. And on 4 November, there wasn't a single banner asking for reunification."

People demanded, envisioned for a second, their own separate land, their own lives, their own hard-won language.

Now the voices are gone, the banners forgotten, and the fleeting sense of community, of self-determined nationhood, that emerged in a fragile articulation from the rallies is withered and swept aside, detritus of an empty autumn. Helmut never truly belonged to the GDR and will not easily fit into the new united Germany. He feels lost, deracinated, a homeless wanderer pining for 4 November. Citizen of a country that only existed for a day, Helmut lives as an exile in a nation of exiles.

"Perhaps we'll go to Australia," he says with a resigned smile. "I really fear the Germans, you know. All I can say is"—and suddenly he is practicing his English—"Lord have mercy, they know not what they do!"

AN UNEASY TRANSFORMATION

"I don't support reunification," Hildegard says, "but I don't know if there is any alternative. My father supports the Christian Democrats because they are the most adamant for reunification. He asked me, 'Do you want to go through this whole shit again?' " She returns to her invariable hobbyhorse, comparative incomes. "We'll never be as rich as they are over there, not even in twenty years."

She too feels the pervasive insecurities of Western life encroaching.

"To be honest with you, I fear reunification. I'm afraid of what's on the other side. As soon as the border was opened, the hectic pace of life in West Berlin took over here also. I'm a little afraid of working on my own, as someone self-employed. It's really important that each person have a certain measure of security. We had the opposite here, too much protection from our own existence. But the drugs and violence and homelessness, that's all coming and I find those things very threatening. West Berlin, too, has problems now that we've created, with their shortage of apartments and crowded schools.

"I'm reading the West German Basic Law, and I know that some things in our constitution are better, but they'll all probably be lost. With unification will come military service—for my sons, I mean. Recently I found out that on this side, they haven't been enforcing military service for the last three to four years. If men just stay home, they haven't been pursuing them. And Gysi along with most of the other party leaders would like to get rid of the draft altogether. But not Kohl!

"Perhaps it doesn't make that much difference," Hildegard reflects bitterly. "We're doomed to becoming the poorest runt of Germany." Then her tone changes and takes on a pensiveness remniscent of Helmut's. "We're all somewhat at a loss for words now."

This impoverishment of East German discourse strikes Hildegard powerfully. It is a society trying to learn how to say things over. Its halting, aphasic way with the newly acquired forms of utterance is apparent in the smallest details. "I went to the parental advisory board of the school recently. The chair didn't know how to address us. She began, 'Frau, Comrades, Herrn and Frauen.' Finally she began to stutter. She couldn't decide which form of address to use, and apologized, saying she had to find a new way of speaking.

"At that meeting we changed three things in the school. We did away with parental advisory commissions, because they hadn't been working. We eliminated the paramilitary organization for children, which was supposed to prepare them for the army. And we agreed that the Democratic Women of Germany organization could continue their contact with our school."

Yet the democratization of school administration has been very difficult to carry out, Hildegard complained. She cited an occasion when each parent was asked to make some suggestion from his or her own experience.

"I was humiliated by four of the women," she said, "when I suggested that the double burden of work and child care was too much for many women, and we couldn't ask mothers to pay more attention to their children's homework. These mothers just don't have the time. I was attacked by women who said they had no problem being both worker and mother and I was not being progressive in my thinking. That took care of that." A defensive array of clichés closed the encounter, as flatly and preemptively as under the old regime. "There was no more discussion."

Another example Hildegard offered of the difficulty in acting democratically was of proposed changes in voting procedures. East Germans are accustomed to voting for candidates as a party slate, not as individuals. At a lengthy meeting of the parental advisory board, democratic procedures were lauded by all speakers, and the joyous opportunity of freely choosing new board members was embraced on all sides. After a few hours of wrangling over exactly how to take advantage of the opportunity, it was decided to vote for a slate instead of for individual members in order to save time. The old ways had their advantages. Everyone had to get home to the children.

Hildegard, meanwhile, is practicing voice. In January 1990 she finally quit her job in the bureaucracy to pursue a full time career as a singer. Her preferred sphere of expression in the Germany to come will be purely aesthetic, entertaining. No more politics for her.

Just before she quit, her company took on two young men who were former members of the Stasi. Forgive and forget, she figured. A month before these men had been universally reviled, but whatever crimes they had committed could hardly matter in a world that moved so quickly, where sins slipped in a matter of weeks into the void of advancing amnesia. Even in the new, cleansed, rebaptized Germany, it might be advantageous to have them around. They had know-how. While the country loses itself in melodramatic recrimination, Hildegard feels, this kind of person will keep quietly controlling the bureaucracy for a long time.

AND AN EASY TRANSFORMATION

Arnim has a hard time thinking of himself as a capitalist. He would rather rank himself with proletarian heroes like Karl Liebknecht, Rosa Luxemburg, and Ernst Thälmann, prewar leaders of the German Communist party. Liebknecht and Luxemburg were brutally murdered by police during the Weimar period; Thälmann was killed in a concentration camp during the Third Reich. Still his idols today, they were the Robin Hoods of his adolescent aspirations.

"I want a world that is more just," he says, "where we protect the weak and support the interests of the common man."

He identifies most with Timur, the childhood hero of several generations of GDR children. The "Timur movement," based on a character in the novel *Timur and His Gang* by Soviet author Arkadi Gaidar, was the animating force behind the Ernst Thälmann Pioneer organization for GDR children. Timur stood for all the best qualities of a young Communist. A cross between a Bolshevik Boy Scout and an ideologically trained Hardy Boy, he went through his adventures selflessly serving others, especially the elderly and the poor.

Armin recited to me a passage from another book, a passage every person raised in the GDR probably knows by heart. The book is *How Steel Is Made Hard*, a novel by Nikolai Ostrowski. The hero, young Pavel Kortschagin, is hungry and ill-clothed. His friends are plagued by epidemics; his work is sabotaged by foreign agents.

"The most valuable thing that a person possesses is life," Pavel declaims. "He is given but a single one. And he should use it so that his years are not wasted without purpose, so that he will not burn from shame for a base and mean past, so that when he dies he may say: my whole life, all of my strength, I have dedicated to the most splendid thing in the world, to the fight for the emancipation of mankind."

History has fooled Arnim, however. Suckled on socialist realist fantasies, weaned on the pap of proletarian fiction, he finds himself in a country rushing headlong into the embrace of capitalism, casting away as adolescent pipe dreams its socialist aspirations and the admonitory examples of Timur and Pavel.

Or has Arnim fooled history? He hasn't been crushed by the great chiasmus. On the contrary, he has flourished. Of all my acquaintances in East Berlin, Arnim was the first to get a job working for a capitalist firm in West Berlin.

Nothing could have been less expected. In the three

years I'd known him, Arnim was the friend who worked the least and drank the most. He showed only the most fleeting interest in "the material world." He had an air of never having fully entered into communion with that world, the sleepy, abstracted air of an agnostic in church. It was something that always puzzled me, until Arnim told me the story of the baptism he'd undergone in 1945.

Arnim has an amazing memory for details that goes back all the way to the last year of the war. He was five years old. His father, a high-ranking SS officer, met his end in 1943 on a battlefield near Moscow. Arnim has a picture of himself from about that time, dressed like Daddy in a little uniform, standing erect and at attention, in one hand a rifle larger than himself, the other holding a flag emblazoned with a swastika.

In January 1945, heavy Allied bombing finally forced his mother to evacuate the family—his brother and himself—from Berlin.

"We were in the basement of a neighbor's house. The neighborhood bomb shelter. There was constant bombing and soldiers were everywhere. If a bomb had hit us, we would have all died under the rubble anyway. Sitting in the basement was no real protection. But that was all beside the point. Only one bomb hit that area in the several years that Berlin was bombed, and it was probably one left over from a Berlin raid that the Allies had forgotten to drop. Anyhow, my mother said we'd waited long enough; it was time to return to our farmhouse."

So they left for what seemed the relative safety of Mecklenburg, eighty miles north of Berlin. "I remember seeing naked men taking the uniforms off of dead soldiers in the street and putting them on. I asked my mother what that was all about. She said the Red Army was coming. I only realized much later that the SS men were exchanging their own uniforms for those of normal soldiers. They knew what they were in for if caught in those [SS] uniforms.

"There were airplanes flying around above us and we heard shooting everywhere. We saw soldiers running in the fields. My mother thought she should find some shelter for myself and my brother, and she'd go on alone to the farmhouse. She stopped at the next house. It belonged to a high-ranking SS officer she knew. We called him uncle, but he wasn't really our uncle. All the men in my family were high-ranking Nazis—grandfather a field marshal, my father an SS officer, my uncle a Nazi party functionary.

"She knocked on the door. Nobody answered. The next day we found out that he had shot his wife and three children, then himself. Can you imagine? If we'd arrived just a few hours earlier, my mother would have left us there, and he would have killed my brother and myself too.

"The next morning," Arnim says calmly, "my mother took my brother and me to a deep ravine and tried to drown us. You've heard of Goebbels' propaganda that the Russians would kill us brutally. He encouraged people to take their own lives. The water was cold and dirty. And I kicked and screamed as she tried to hold me under. She wasn't the only mother to try that. You know, many women first killed their children, then themselves."

Arnim told all of this matter-of-factly. He is a handsome man who looks more like thirty than fifty, with a wonderful sense of humor. He is gay and during the time I knew him, up to autumn 1989, he whiled away his days in public toilets, his evenings in corner bars. Only when he related this story did I understand his outstanding peculiarity: his adamant refusal to bathe. Arnim's aversion to water had always been a subject of fun, and of some alarm, among his friends. A mutual friend scolded him and poured bathwater for him when he visited. Behind a closed door, Arnim would splash around with his hands, to deceive us that he was bathing. He rarely so much as washed. His smell became so strong that it was difficult to stand in a room with him. Anyone could tell with eyes closed that Arnim was coming. I myself started to avoid him.

Sauberkeit, cleanliness, is something quintessentially German. With order and discipline, it forms a holy trinity of anal-retentive national traits. Arnim lacked all three. I assumed his slovenliness and smell were a form of protest, an ingrained reaction against the German ideal, until he told me how his mother tried to drown him.

During my fieldwork, I heard many stories about the bravery and strength of German women. They are rightfully credited with saving the lives of their children (and husbands when they returned from the prisoner-of-war camps) from the abyss of physical and moral defeat in 1945 through extraordinary personal sacrifices and ingenious economies and dealings. Their remarkable dedication preserved discipline and order amid the disaster. But Arnim remembers his mother's strength in a different light. He vividly remembers the ravine. The image haunts him in his dreams. He sees himself crawling out of the ravine, mud-soaked, baptized, enrolled in a cruel community of adulthood and death.

Arnim seemed to function well until the late 1970s. True, he had a chip on his shoulder, but he hid it well. As a bright, promising youth of eighteen, in 1958 he had been accepted into the Socialist Unity party at a time when membership was hard to attain, when only the ideologically committed and talented youth, like Timur and his gregarious gang, were taken into the ranks. In 1974 he had a fight with his local party secretary, calling her a "dogmatic cow." She had him kicked out of the party.

He had always held demanding jobs. He worked in the same fashion and design business his grandfather had founded and his father had carried on before the war. It had long since been taken over by the state, but Arnim was perversely proud of that. He wasn't interested in owning property. It sufficed that he had inherited a feel for the business from his family, which helped him contribute to clothing—and building—the socialist society. He retained a stubborn sense of integrity. Around 1977, his boss was investigated for smuggling, leading eventually to his arrest and imprisonment. Arnim was the only employee who refused to testify against him.

And then, suddenly, he just stayed home. He lost three jobs in succession. One day, he would simply refuse to get up. For the next few weeks he would not open the door to his apartment. His employers came to visit him—a responsibility assigned them by the GDR, which expected firms to look after their employees. But Arnim's supervisors could never determine whether he was actually there. Arnim locked the doors, turned off the heat and electricity to save money, and slept away the days. For nutrition, he ate carrots; they were cheap and good for the teeth. After eleven in the evening, when his neighbors were asleep, he sneaked out to the local bars to drink beer with his buddies. He lived on his savings. Because rents and food prices were heavily subsidized in East Germany, a little money went a long way and he could always borrow from friends if things got bad. So long as he didn't engage in any "political crime," the state left him alone, happily free, unemployed, and unwashed.

No particular event or experience brought Arnim to the

point where he wouldn't work. Each time, it just seemed to happen. One fine morning he could no longer summon the will to throw off the covers and rub his eyes. If this had happened under capitalism, Arnim would hardly have been able to subsist, much less recover. Once a career trajectory in capitalism begins a downward slope, it rarely reverses itself. Careers in a capitalist society tend to follow linear paths. Employers take little protective responsibility for their workers. Their only duty is to pay them and their primary concern is to discipline them. Moreover, in a market society, however wide its safety net is spread, the loss of a job often means the loss of living space. Without an income, rent money is hard to find. Disasters under capitalism never come singly. The loss of sustained earning power leads quickly to other losses, which batter and defeat the victim irremediably. In East Germany, by contrast, it was almost unheard-of for tenants to lose their apartments, least of all for unpaid rent.

Curled in fetal position on his bed, carrots in one hand, bottle in the other, this Beckettian figure in shabby clothes was perhaps the GDR's ideal citizen, pure product of its norms. He had responded to an environment of lack and encoded deprivation by reducing his needs to a daily portion of alcohol and his life to a politically neutered self-destructiveness. He had responded to a culture of fear by closing himself in the safe silence of his room. His public life shrank to drunken stupors in neighborhood bars, while his private life of fantasy and dream burgeoned in harmless isolation.

The petrified time of the East suited him well. He need never hurry. Time was the one kind of capital he had in limitless quantities, to waste, spend, give. He was the perfectly passive recipient of state largesse, the citizen who couldn't possibly give offense, the absolutely reliable man. Arnim even felt that he was fulfilling his productive capacities. He produced fantasies. He was a doer and what he did was dream. Dream and drink. He got smashed. Daily. He drank and forgot everything as fast as he experienced it. In his self-created, self-canceling, self-centered world, time stood still.

"He has no sense of time," his friends would say when he was—as always—late for meetings. "Probably spent last night in the bars and overslept." I remember time spent with him as a maze of missed appointments and misunderstandings. With nothing else to fill his days, he liked to run errands for friends. He ran an errand once in preparation for one of my two-day visits to the East in 1988 (I was living in West Berlin at the time) scheduled to begin officially at 6:00 A.M. on Monday and end at 10:00 P.M. on Tuesday. The friend with whom I was to stay had asked Arnim to do some shopping the Saturday before my arrival. He had to work on Saturday when the stores were open and didn't want to greet me with an empty cupboard. Arnim agreed to meet my friend early Saturday to discuss what to buy. He never showed up.

"Typical Arnim," my friend fulminated. Outraged at such irresponsibility, he hung a sharply worded note on his door before going to work. The note began with the greeting "L.A.," shorthand for *Lieber Arnim* (Dear Arnim), and in the second line accused Arnim of being *was für ein Arsch* (some kind of an ass). Arnim showed up several hours later with groceries he'd selected on his own, special breads from a private bakery, smoked ham and salami from a butcher friend, cheeses from a *Delikat* shop. Glancing at the note, Arnim associated the greeting "L.A." with the *"Arsch"* from the second line, and inferred that Wolfgang, our mutual friend, meant not *Lieber Arnim*, but *Leck mich am Arsch* (lick my ass). Humiliated and furious, Arnim scribbled *Unsinn* (nonsense) under the note, followed by a stream of insults. Another friendship broken, another mistake to repair some other day.

His nights were a wildly varied succession of erotic adventures that somehow always managed to seem monotonous. One week he spent every night cruising the public toilets around the Friedrichshain park. In the morning, he emerged to have coffee and read the papers in the café near the huge sculpture of Lenin. At that time, Arnim had donned a new leather look. He shaved his thick hair and began wearing tight leather pants, a black leather jacket, and black boots. His entrance into the café was met by scandalized stares.

One bright dawn, as he sat armored in leather, reading *Neues Deutschland*, the official party newspaper, a waitress asked if he knew how he looked. He said no. She advised him to take a look in the mirror.

In the bathroom, Arnim discovered his face was as black as a coal miner's. During the night, he had met another leather queen who asked Arnim to lick his boots. Obviously, something had rubbed off. Arnim washed the black off as best he could, then returned to his table and read the paper as if nothing had changed, oblivious to stares. To the waitress, who approached him again to take his order, he merely commented that he had been to a masquerade and hadn't yet washed his face paint off. Such peccadilloes were the stuff of his life until the autumn of 1989.

Suddenly everything changed. All at once, whether moved by the residual stirrings of ambition, by the greedy atmosphere of the GDR as a whole, or by the general air of change that suffused everything, he rose from bed early. Something was happening to him. He sought out a job, in a cinema. In November he declared he had a mission: he would devote his life to the renewal of socialist society. Several months later a different kind of opportunity opened.

After eight years in prison, his former boss at the fashion house had been released to the West. Once in West Berlin, the man founded a clothing design business. Soon after the opening of the Wall he contacted Arnim and told his loyal ex-employee that he had never forgotten Arnim's refusal to give incriminating testimony against him. He asked the unwashed, disheveled Arnim to work as the chief sales representative throughout Germany for his flourishing firm.

At first, Arnim refused. "I can't drive. I'd kill myself if I had to drive from city to city; I just can't do that." But his former boss pressed hard. He needed an employee who could be fully trusted. The West Germans didn't want to work particularly hard and they wanted too much money. He sweetened the terms.

"He offered me the job just for Berlin. And I agreed. What the hell, it's a good offer." In mid-February, Arnim went to work for his old boss. There were a few conditions. He must agree to bathe regularly, cut his fingernails and clean his hands, and get his teeth taken care of (he had lost several incisors in barroom fights).

Amazingly, Arnim complied. Since then, he has been sober, *sauber,* and a diligent worker. He demonstrated an astonishing pliancy, in fact, a childlike willingness to be led into the confusing, exotic new world of wonders beyond the Wall. More than most other GDR citizens, Arnim was ripe for the comic twist of the revolution. His life had been pure farce and now he was finally, at the age of fifty, in step with history. His own story was one of escape, repression, sublimation. He had long lived in his own world of withdrawal—what the Germans call an "inner emigration." Yet the childishness of his responses to East German experience helped him endure the shock of discovering the West. Because he had no sophisticated expectations, no world of social norms to be shattered and remade, no complicated codes of behavior or discourse to be unlearned, the new frame of reference didn't disturb him as it did his hapless compatriots. Socialism had made him a paradigm of passivity, waiting to be seized in rapture and swept away. The great overweening West had only to take him by the hand.

Whether Arnim can couple his willingness to learn with a capacity to make informed choices and seize the initiative; whether he can counter his imperturbable acceptance of the new order of things with an earnest, arduous eagerness to muscle others out and grab his share; whether, in the long run, he can make the adjustments necessary to survive under a capitalist system remains to be seen. By being, in many ways, a better socialist citizen than his alternately grousing and excitable fellows, by fulfilling the state's ideal of satiety and safety, locked in fantasy and in his four-walled womb, Arnim unwittingly better prepared himself to take the first hard step toward capitalism.

This once and future clothes salesman made the transition from one infantilizing system to another with almost seamless ease. His long retreat from the demands of a death-obsessed adulthood, which had its origin in that quicksilver morning in the ice-cold ravine, prepared him admirably for a place in our postmodern society, where change is the only constant and evasion is the one fixed rule. His long fight to forget armored him for a world of amnesia. Socialism readied him to obey one of the fundamental commands of a capitalist society addicted to distractions: *you shall become as little children....* You must be born again, the world told Arnim. And he was.

9

Transitions:
Crossing the Wall

What is this furniture
That speaks of departure?
—Gunter Grass, *Folding Chairs*

A CONTINENT ON THE MOVE

Suddenly, in the twentieth century, settled, stolid Europe—the home of bourgeois civilization, the cradle of ideologized private property—became a continent of nomads. Caught between intolerable pasts and unknowable futures, incalculable hordes of people trekked across the boundaries of states. Over the years between 1918 and 1945, and especially at the end of the Second World War, population transfers to rival any in world history were imposed, often by force, on the map of Europe. During the war alone, 60 million Europeans were displaced. The suffering and death caused by these mass exiles and migrations were exorbitant. It is both a tribute to, and a terrifying commentary on, modern civilization that their memory is so effectively repressed in the glittering, seemingly eternal, skyscraper cities of Western Europe, so many of which are founded on the bones of the displaced.

Mass relocations of Germans have been a signal feature of this lamentable history. Over 6.5 million so-called "ethnic Germans" were deported from East and Northeast Europe after 1945, in an "ethnic cleanup" performed by the Allies in accord with the Potsdam agreement. From 1944 to 1961 nearly 12 million Germans fled the former territories of the *Ostgebiete*, which had been ceded to Poland and the Soviet Union. Germans bereft of their onetime Germany, these refugees at one point made up nearly one-quarter of all the people in what are now the Federal Republic and the GDR. Their integration played a major role in the process of postwar German identity building.[1]

Against such enormous relocations, the scurrying movements recently disturbing the two Germanies may seem insignificant, a mere digestive disturbance. Under 350,000 citizens left the GDR for West Germany even in 1953, the year of the great worker uprising, eight years before the Wall was in place. The year before the Wall was built, refugees totaled less than 220,000. However, the psychological disturbances of relocating—to a country admittedly still Germany, but an Alice-in-Wonderland Germany, beyond the looking glass—have been immense for many former East Germans resettled in the West over the past four decades. Overcoming the divide has been an earthshaking effort for such refugees. Rarely has the transition been easy. Their experiences are part of the repressed history of the Cold War. One must consider closely the tales of displacement and reintegration these Germans on the move have to tell.

This chapter centers on the stories of Klaus and Franziska. Headstrong Klaus, born in 1955, was one of the last East Germans to experience the crossing of the border as a transgression. He came to West Berlin by way of Hungary in 1989, shortly before the Wall opened. In contrast, Franziska was fifteen and much less conscious of the overarching significance of the act when she and her mother came West in 1987. In different ways they have encountered the problem of deriving a coherent sense of self from the dissevered and disparate events they endured in two radically unassimilable worlds.

Both stories are, in a sense, of failure. Neither Klaus or Franziska is fully satisfied with the patched-together values they have woven from the incompatible halves of their lives. Other, more enduring walls greeted both when they crossed the Wall. Klaus and Franziska's accounts may serve to suggest some of the difficulties that await the German body politic as it stitches itself together, reassembling its scattered limbs and heralding, perhaps prematurely, its longed-for oneness.

PARADISE LOST

One afternoon in September of 1988, I arrived at the apartment of an East Berlin friend to find him distraught. His best friend, Klaus, had just telephoned him—from West Berlin. Klaus had gone to Hungary on vacation. Once there, apparently on impulse, he had joined the mass exodus of

East Germans taking advantage of the newly porous Hungarian border to escape to Austria, then to West Germany. "I just bet he got carried away there," my friend said, "seeing all the others leave. He got caught up in the hysteria of the moment and just went with the others. But I can't believe it," he added, venting deep feelings of frustration and betrayal. "He'd never said one word to me. You don't realize what this means to me. I have only one other friend left here. He was really the only person with whom I could discuss everything."

His resentment was as nothing to that voiced by the woman who was the real victim of Klaus's flight, Marianne, Klaus's wife. She had been on her own, separate, vacation when her husband defected to the West. She claimed she had no idea her husband was planning an escape.

Everyone seemed horrified by Klaus's rash act. When Marianne broke the news to Klaus's working-class parents, they were shattered. Weeping, they protested that they couldn't believe it. Hadn't they done everything their only child had ever asked? Hadn't they fixed up his apartment, bought him a new Czech car, brought him books from the West when he needed them? They denied him nothing. He had a good job, was paid very well, had prestige, got along with his colleagues. As he was a rising star at his institute, he would soon be able to travel legally in the West. They couldn't understand why he left. Why now? What was wrong?

I knew Klaus and Marianne fairly well. Both were beautiful people, young, intelligent, and successful. They weren't of the manicured beauty one finds in West Berlin, where clothes make the man and makeup makes the woman, where a fine ripe sheen of money rounds out beauty like a halo, where a new hairstyle and a Majorca tan during the winter give one the necessary touch of distinction. They had unassuming, unkempt good looks, which they did nothing special to embellish. Marianne, a Czech citizen, taught philosophy at the Institute for Marxism-Leninism and Klaus worked at a research institute as a sociolinguist, pursuing research on the relationship between *Schein* and *Sein*, appearance and being. They had been married for six years.

Klaus was a very abstract, *unsinnlich* person. On the street or on the train, or faced with a menu or a landscape, he never seemed to notice the things around him. He seemed always to be burrowing in his imagination beneath the deceptions of appearance for some elemental, verbal truth. His indifference to the material world was enabled in part by the degree to which his needs were always satisfied. An only child of a working-class family, he was his parents' darling, a coddled and indulged child. His wants, in any case, were relatively limited, his primary needs abstract ones, for books and music, artifacts of high culture easily obtained in the East.

Marianne, the mortified and abandoned wife, was by far the more plausible candidate for sudden flight. She had complex, shifting needs. My friend described her as a *Schmetterling*, a butterfly who liked to be noticed. Her talents were many. She excelled at anything she tried, from athletic endeavors to playing musical instruments. Perhaps because everything was so easy for her, she took nothing very seriously. She loved fine things: fashionable furniture, the latest music, good foods, and fancy wines.

Why had Klaus fled? No one could decide. No one knew the real truth underlying the appearance of sudden, impulsive escape. Klaus wasn't like the overwhelmed and unprepared vacationers, the unhappy campers who took off on a whim across the new gap in the rusting iron curtain. He wasn't one of the muddled thousands who elected at the last minute to cross the border into Austria and the unknown. Klaus had it all planned out. And Marianne was his accomplice. They had considered carefully how best to make their break, perfecting their plans for a month, confiding in no one. He would go first, taking advantage of the open border. Then Marianne, a Czech, for whom legal egress would be much more difficult under ordinary circumstances, would ask to follow, using the powerful argument that she had a right to be reunited with her husband on the other side.

Perhaps Marianne, anxious to taste a consumer culture denied her in drab East Berlin, had talked him into it. Yet I suspect Klaus was moved more by a dialectic not dissimilar to the one he pursued in his rarefied research. The West had always existed for him as pure *Schein*, a glimmering succession of images and shadows on a one-dimensional screen, inaccessible picture perfect pleasure. Somewhere beneath those airy appearances, he knew, was the flesh and blood of a real West, with geography, body, truth. To discover such a truth, he crossed the dissolving border.

Marianne followed to the letter the plans she had made with Klaus. At the institute where she worked, she bemoaned his desertion to her sympathetic colleagues. What could she do? She complained and wept, berating the absent Klaus for leaving without saying a word. While she was on vacation! She was a foreigner here in the GDR and had no desire to stay on alone. Yet she had no future in Czechoslovakia either. Marianne is a capable actress. Her colleagues comforted her. She shouldn't worry, they would help her get by.

Meanwhile, Marianne quickly prepared for her own move. She gave away most of their furniture, much of their large, valued record collection, and sold their new Czech car. She thought she would have no problem taking the rest of their belongings with her to West Berlin. When she tried to cross the border the following week, however, armed with explanations and proof of her husband's desertion, the GDR border guard told her she needed a visa from the Czech embassy before he could allow her to travel to the West.

Undaunted (she had expected bureaucratic obstacles) she went to the Czech embassy on Otto-Grotewohl Strasse the next day. She played the abandoned wife to the fullest, insisting she wanted only to get her man back. The officials impassively informed her that they could not give her a visa. Marriage or no marriage, as a Czech citizen she would have to go back to Czechoslovakia and request one there.

"I've lived here for six years," she pleaded, tears and trills flowing in an impromptu aria worthy of Menotti's *Consul*, "I am a permanent resident here, my husband has left me."

The motionless marble faces repeated their monosyllabic noes.

She went to Prague where she explained her situation to official after official. Deserted wife; sanctity of marriage; right to pursue deceitful man. The refrain echoed in cobwebbed vaults. The bureaucrats responded that it was possible to issue her a visa, but not directly. First they would have to investigate her story. She might have to wait a couple of months or more. In the meantime, they said, she should return to Czechoslovakia to live; it would be best to wait near the center of authority.

Instead, Marianne went back to East Berlin, not knowing what to do. Her colleagues grew concerned about her. They came to visit in the evening, bringing her baked goods. She greeted them with a blank look worthy of a bureaucrat, a dazed indifferent smile. They understood. She wasn't the first person to have lost a spouse under such circumstances. Everyone knew of someone who had lost a close friend or relative to the "Golden West."

Marianne conferred with Klaus on the telephone. What should she do? He suggested she move to Czechoslovakia and wait for her visa. She didn't trust his advice. She didn't seem to trust anyone anymore. All these events had infected her with a comprehensive uncertainty. One day on the telephone, she accused Klaus of having left her. Why didn't he come back?

"But Marianne," he said, trying not to incriminate her on the telephone, for he was sure their conversation was being overheard, "you know I can't return."

She refused to believe him. He was in the real West, the world of *Sein*, and he had betrayed her to live in a nightmare of perpetual and deceitful appearance. She was battering her head against a television screen, while flickering faces waved and smiled.

Several days later, Marianne's colleagues took her to the hospital and checked her into the psychiatric ward. She was confused, babbling. Her husband had left and run to West Berlin. He had deserted her in the GDR and gone to live in the TV. She refused to talk with her friends and colleagues anymore, accusing them of betraying her as her husband had done. She hated the TV in her hospital room.

Three weeks later, the Wall was opened and Klaus could travel back to the GDR. He began visiting Marianne three times a week in the hospital.

His new life in West Berlin was not going according to

plan. *Sein* was hard to come by in the neon glow of West Berlin. Appearances multiplied, as did betrayals of the golden dream. He had hoped that his two university degrees would be quickly recognized, clearing the way to a faculty appointment, but university authorities refused his requests. Matters might be different, they remarked, if he had studied in a regular philosophy department, but his studies, though in the respectable field of sociolinguistics, had been at an Institute of Marxism-Leninism. Such degrees are not recognized in West Germany.

Klaus was devastated by their denial of the validity and worth of his hard-won pieces of paper. He began muttering that he didn't really care about studying anymore, it wasn't what he wanted to do with his life. He got an interim job as a ticket collector in a theater, and that, he decided contemptuously, suited him quite well for the moment. Soon he would find something better, work where he could earn more money. That was his real goal, he contended. It was where true Being seemed to lie in the West—earning money, living well.

Soon even work lost its attractions. After three months in West Berlin, Klaus quit his job and moved back into the apartment in East Berlin with Marianne (released from the hospital, but still stunned). As a registered *Flüchtling* or refugee in West Berlin, he qualifies for an array of social welfare benefits: unemployment compensation for several years, subsidized rent, a subsidized rail pass, and free health care. As long as the authorities in West Berlin do not discover his return to the East (difficult to prove in the flux following the border opening), he should continue doing well on state support.

He has become, in fact, a new, 1990s brand of *Grenzgänger*. The term *Grenzgänger* became popular in the 1950s to describe individuals who lived in one side of the city but worked in the other. The vast majority of border crossers were East Germans living in the rent- and food-subsidized East and earning the valuable deutschmark by working in the West. This arrangement—capitalist earnings, socialist care—made them wealthy in comparison to their fellow citizens, both East and West. They were entrepeneurs of a sort, taking advantage of political division to enhance their economic position, shuttling on a busy loom constructed by the Cold War, working hard and spending freely.

After the building of the Wall, the phenomenon disintegrated, save for an infinitesimal number of officially approved exceptions. After the opening of the Wall, *Grenzgänger* reappeared practically overnight. Klaus, however, is a novel variation on the phenomenon, a *Grenzgänger* without initiative, sapped of energy. He no longer works. He dreams a lot and collects benefits on one side of the border. He has, in effective, switched from one system of dependency to another.

His life and Marianne's were deformed by the intolerable circumstance of the walled division across East German experience. They felt lopped, stunted, by their perceived imprisonment in the East. Their lives seeming unreal and empty, they looked for an idealized reality somewhere beyond the border or the TV screen. That other reality eluded their grasp. Politics barred Marianne from it when she thought it was at hand. Klaus found, even on the other side, satiety slipping away. Now suspended between two worlds, they inhabit an ambiguous compromise, half-here, half-there, nowhere really, in a taut utopia of dreams, walking the tightrope between a disappearing world and one that is all appearance.

BREAKING OUT

I first met Franziska in November 1986, at the home of her mother, Beate, during my first stay in East Berlin. I was living in an apartment "leased" by Humboldt University in a building owned by the National People's Army. The building had an exotic mix of residents. In the elevator I might meet a linguist from France, physicians from Lebanon and Syria, or a nuclear physicist from Bulgaria, as well as the ubiquitous GDR soldiers in blue-gray, ill-fitting uniforms, stone-faced, forbidden to talk to me. My next-door neighbor, a Burmese man, taught Burmese at Humboldt University. One day he asked if I'd like to tutor in English a family he knew. I demurred, but he insisted. They were good people to know, he said, especially the mother, who knew "anybody who was somebody in the GDR." I finally agreed to give it a try.

In the end I visited Beate and Franziska about two evenings a month, to speak English with a small group of their friends. Franziska always appeared with her cousin, a stunningly beautiful black girl of the same age whose mother was a German doctor and father, I was told, an African from Mozambique. Franziska inherited from her father a solid Russian peasant's body and blond German hair. She was well behaved, an almost prototypical East German girl, self-effacing but confident, secure but without a perceptible sense of self-satisfaction. I never saw this type of youth in West Berlin, where the arrogance of wealth and comfort (West Berlin, despite its relative poverty vis-à-vis West Germany, was an oasis of material goods in a desert of threadbare socialism) produced youths who, in proportion as they were content, were also closed, smug, and uncritical. At that time Franziska seemed to be hungering for something, but unable to articulate what.

Franziska's parents, Beate and Walter, had known each other since their days as high school sweethearts in Dresden. Beate's father was a doctor in Hitler's army. He was taken prisoner by the Russians and resettled in Dresden after his release. He left his first wife and four children to marry a nurse 20 years his junior who bore him Beate and another daughter. Walter is a not-uncommon product of the postwar situation in East Germany. His mother, a German woman, had an affair with a Russian soldier during the occupation immediately after the end of the war. The soldier returned to Leningrad and 11 years later she married a Yugoslav. She maintained contact with her Russian lover, however, and Walter later visited his paternal grandmother in Leningrad several times.

When I first met her, Beate worked as a neurologist at the East Berlin Charite Hospital. Walter was unemployed—a situation semantically as well as financially delicate, since at that time "unemployed" people did not officially exist in the GDR—but not because he couldn't find a job. He had worked as a salesman in an engineering firm. In 1985 he quit his job and applied to leave the GDR, having reached the limits of what he could earn and what money could buy for him there. When I met him he had spent eighteen months waiting for government approval to depart.

The wait could be endless. Walter doggedly stuck to official channels, refusing to take the course many would-be emigrants regarded as surest; committing a crime that could be seen as political in West Germany. Arrest and imprisonment would follow and registration of these acts by the

West German authorities, who maintained a secret shopping list of East German dissidents, a sort of bargain-basement treasury of grace and merit. The West Germans would buy the freedom of the jailed dissenter, usually within two years, though it could take much longer.

The first such exchange of West German money for GDR citizens was a relatively spontaneous barter after the 1953 protests in the East. Later the trades became a regularized part of German/German relations. People to be exchanged were put on two lists: political prisoners ("H-Cases") and family members of West German citizens ("F-Cases").

Walter was ultimately exchanged in 1989, without having to sully his record with a political crime. The number of family-related exchanges had been steadily increasing relative to the political exchanges. In 1965, there were 1,555 H-Cases and 762 F-Cases. In 1975, the number of H-Cases had dropped to 1,158 while the number of F-Cases increased to 5,635. In 1989, the H-Cases numbered 1,775, while F-Cases had risen to 69,447. Altogether, from 1965 to 1989, 33,755 "political prisoners" and 215,019 "family members" were bought. The price went up over time, reaching approximately 20,000 deutschmarks per person ($12,000) by 1977.

Neither regime could discuss the bodies-for-money exchanges. Bartering humans like baseball cards was in blatant violation of international law and publicizing the system would have had serious domestic repercussions on both sides. It was common knowledge among East German citizens, however, whispered with a mixture of gratitude and humiliation, that their richer siblings in the West were shopping for their lives.

Walter had made his decision to leave East Germany

unilaterally, without consulting his family. It caused considerable strain on the marriage. Beate's original stupefied neutrality hardened gradually into a definite preference for staying in the GDR.

Beate had married young. She was only twenty-one when Franziska was born and very much in love with Walter. That love had long since cooled and Beate had grown more self-confident and assertive. Earlier, she had looked up to father figures. Her own father had been a domineering character, her mother a *Nurhausfrau*, just a housewife in the common East German phrase, who had lived only to serve her husband's needs. Walter was solid, steady, a "good fatherly type," but Franziska was grown now, and Beate was an independent professional with a life of her own. Neither one, Beate felt, needed a father in the house any more.

Beate was a budding intellectual with an enormous library. At least half her books were not published in the GDR. Friends were always smuggling in books for her. She ran a sort of circulating library, lending her books to all her friends. A volume might go through ten to thirty readings before returning to her. As a neurologist, wife, and mother, Beate probably had less spare time than many Western intellectuals. She had, however, a community of hungry fellow readers who expected her to read and to discuss what she had read.

Walter, on the other hand, was mainly interested in following European soccer tournaments or the latest elections in West Germany. Nobody in the East took an interest in their own politicians, but many knew all the names and positions of West German politicians. Walter was another television addict, dazedly watching the doings of the West behind the glass cage of the TV.

In a familiar pattern, Franziska became a bone of contention between her parents' increasingly divergent interests. Beate encouraged Franziska to read and think critically. Walter wanted her to relax and take it easy. When I first met Franziska, she liked to do both. Her lively critical intelligence was focused on after-school activities, while she made her lazy and slipshod way through school.

What really broke up the marriage, Beate explained to me, was the crucial question of whether to have another child or her third abortion. Since 1972, abortion in the GDR has been not only legal, but provided as part of the government health care system. With Franziska on the verge of adulthood, Beate had come to a turning point in her life. She welcomed her unplanned pregnancy with all the familiar fervor of a middle-aged person dreaming of a second chance. She longed to give another child the love and attention she felt she had only doled out stintingly to Franziska, "because I was too young, too inexperienced, too busy with my education and career."

When she told Walter she was pregnant again, he dismissed her desire to have a child. Children were valuable to the GDR, which promoted parenthood to compensate for the population drain to the West. A newborn baby would complicate Walter's application to emigrate. He urged her to have an abortion.

"He showed no concern for what it meant to me," she complained. Some last, intangible barrier broke within her. Beate decided to divorce Walter.

A rush of other decisions followed. Once divorce proceedings were started, Beate elected to have the abortion after all; the strain of being a single mother would be too great. Abruptly, she made another momentous choice. She would go West, as Walter had wanted all along. Since she was starting all over again, as an unmarried professional, why not do it in the land of second chances? Curiously, in the very act of emotionally distancing herself from her stolid husband, she mimicked his choices. She *became* him or at least what he had wanted her to be. It was (she would reflect later) as though the very acts meant to affirm her freedom left her puzzlingly less free.

Franziska fought the divorce with all the means at her disposal, with tantrums and threats to leave both parents and live with a friend. Walter resisted the divorce, and when his wife refused reconciliation, threatened to go to court to keep his daughter. For a time the air was thick with threats and counterthreats, accusations and insults. Walter was only dissuaded from a custody battle when Beate reminded him that a daughter in his household would hold up his petition to emigrate. Franziska herself preferred staying with Walter.

"My father was much more tolerant with me than Beate. He didn't criticize me for getting bad grades, and he had a lot more time for me than my mother did. In the end, I'm glad I stayed with Beate. She always had more interesting friends, many intellectuals, and that has left its impression on me over time."

Beate, meanwhile, arranged her exit through remarriage. First she quit her job at the Charité and began working part-time for a Christian organization. People in critical occupations, such as doctors, found it more difficult to emigrate than others. Professionals were continually bleeding away from the GDR, attracted by the higher pay in West Germany and the higher social status in a hierarchical, nonproletarian society. The regime would do anything to stop them. By abandoning her profession, Beate hoped to make herself a less desirable commodity to the state. Next, she contacted an old boyfriend from her Dresden days, now living in West Berlin. He arranged for her to meet a West German artist, who agreed to a marriage of convenience.

Since the GDR and FRG were separate countries (at least according to GDR law; in 1987, West Germany finally recognized the East German state but still disputed its citizenship claims), East German citizens had to get approval to marry a "foreigner," a category that naturally included West Berliners. The government, alert to aspirations of escape, rejected Beate's initial petition to marry her West Berlin friend. Thwarted in her first attempt, Beate asked an old friend, attorney Gregor Gysi, to represent her. At the time, Gysi was head of the union representing all GDR defense attorneys. In two years he would become the postrevolutionary head of the Communist party.

She had met Gysi five years before at a private party, at a time when she was trying to switch jobs in the hospital from an experimental station to a full-time neurology division. Stymied by her superiors, particularly by the doctor in charge, who claimed he needed her services where she was, she appealed the issue to the local conflict commission, a people's court comprised of employees elected from the work unit.

The conflict commission ruled for Beate, and with the aid of Gysi's aggressive defense, the decision was upheld on appeal in the district and federal courts. Her coworkers later told me they admired her courage in defending the decision. It later became easier to switch jobs at the Charité, as well as to defend oneself against superiors.

Gysi agreed to counsel her in her latest case. It took less than a year to obtain approval for her marriage. Beate suspects the decision had little to do with the merits of her case, but rather with a West German politician, friendly with Honecker, who interceded on her behalf.

All through the process the state alternately berated and tempted her, switching from carrot to stick in a vain attempt to keep her in the GDR. Interview followed interview, practically until the moment of departure. In the last interview, the official emphasized his personal power to accept or reject her petition. After half an hour of politeness he turned on her, accusing her of poor moral character for leaving, of being a bad worker, of disloyalty to her family and friends who would remain behind.

In the end the petition was granted. The one condition put upon her emigration was that she sign a statement voluntarily renouncing her GDR citizenship. She signed.

WHO IS THE WE?

Franziska and Beate resettled in January 1988. I had moved from East to West Berlin nine months earlier and helped find them an apartment.

At first, Beate was allowed to return to the East for periodic visits, a freedom she found essential to her transition to life in West Berlin. None of her Eastern friends had permission to travel to the West. Moreover, Beate's mother was ill and depended for care on Beate and her sister.

Nevertheless the anxieties caused by her emigration were profound. Beate found herself severed from a whole matrix of relationships. The decision to emigrate had strained Beate's relationship with her sister. By the time she left the GDR, she was no longer on speaking terms with her brother-in-law, a social-climbing party member who demanded personal loyalty to the state. After moving to the West, Beate saw very little of them.

Walter was still in the East. Once in West Berlin, Franziska began to search for ways to get her father out. Untimely ripped from her safe circle of friends and family in the East, feeling adrift and ill-at-ease on this stranded island of West Berlin, she wanted another tangible connection with the past. She tried a number of approaches, writing to Honecker and other East German officials, and even to the industrialist Armand Hammer, about whom she read in a magazine. Nothing helped.

Walter's release in mid-1989 was unconnected to any intercessions on his behalf. The approval of his petition seemed the result of the arcane and unintelligible geological processes, the slow tectonic movements and tellurian shifts which East Germans had learned to accept as the working style of their government.

"Why now?" I asked Walter.

"I don't know," he replied. "You never know what they're doing over there."

Initially Walter moved in with his grandmother in West Germany. Like Beate and Franziska, he was granted permission to visit his friends in the East. For the first three months, he drove the six hours from his home in West Germany to East Berlin every Friday, and drove the six hours back on either Sunday night or Monday. He had finally been allowed to emigrate, the fulfillment of a dream of many years, but he still spent much of his time in East Berlin. Though his work and home had shifted to the West, his heart stayed in the East.

Fearing that the GDR might in the future deny him reentry, Walter took preventive action. He changed his name to the maiden name of his mother. With luck, he might thus escape being registered in the East German computer system and enter the GDR over and over again in perpetuity, as a new man.

Franziska found life in West Berlin very difficult. Even walking down the streets was like being assaulted. The Kurfürstendamm was one long screaming sales pitch, a dissonant symphony of sensory overload. She told me again and again about the initial disorientation and ultimate sense of exhaustion and incompetence she and her mother experienced while shopping. They were enticed into buying things they didn't need or want. Even when shopping for the simplest things, such as marmalade or toothpaste, they had no idea how to discriminate between varieties.

Education was particularly problematic for Franziska. She found the West Berlin Gymnasium where she was studying too difficult, and liked neither the teachers nor the other students.

Nearly a third of her classmates had been born in the GDR and were learning to make the same adjustments she was, yet their common origin did not bring them together as a group. They seemed atomized, at a loss around each other. The pervasive competitiveness and individualism of the school environment divided and baffled them. All the generational experiences specific to the GDR that should have mattered didn't count, or didn't count enough: their highly regulated childhood beginning with preschool at age one, kindergarten, and *Kinderhorte*; their youth activities including membership in the party-regulated Free German Youth. Even their status as refugees or resettlers from a socialist country, and their mutual unfamiliarity with capitalism, did not create a basis for unity, at least not for Franziska.

She tried to integrate with native West Berliners, but

there, too, she found herself separated by a deep gulf. Her politics were different from her classmates'. Several espoused what Franziska termed "right-radical" ideology, directing passionate hatred against the Turks and Poles. She was amazed they could say such things in the classroom, though the teacher herself disapproved of the statements. Franziska declared they would have been severely disciplined, even dismissed, for making comparable comments in an East Berlin school.

Although all her credits from East Berlin were transferable, Franziska felt overprepared for some classes and underprepared for others. She found herself far behind in English, for example. She couldn't follow discussions for the full first year. She took Russian, but found that methods of instruction in West Berlin were different from the East. Her Russian classes in East Berlin had centered around memorization and rote. In the West she found herself forced to express herself spontaneously in Russian. She spluttered, gagged on words, embarrassed herself before the class. She knew the language competently, but in freewheeling, unplanned situations she had no idea what to say.

Her Eastern education had also given her unforeseen strengths. Franziska felt she was a better reader than her Western peers. She could understand and hold in suspension multiple meanings in a text, and catch ironies and parodies with ease. Her West Berlin colleagues could not read between the lines. They sought *Eindeutigkeit*, a single meaning, in the works they read. Franziska was accustomed to seeing layered meanings in everyday life in East Berlin, where some things were spoken about and others not, depending on context and time, where meanings were bred in private places, and homes, rooms, and hearts were zones of fantasy, laboratories for refining the authoritative words of the state.

Junge Welt, for instance, the official youth newspaper of the Communist party, was only interesting if one looked for unintended ironies, was only intelligible if one searched for changes in tone and minor shifts in emphasis, for titles suddenly dropped from party leaders' names or for damnation hidden in faint praise. The party always signaled impending changes in policy without ever *saying* them. Things always signified more than they appeared to.

By contrast, in the West private fantasies were colonized by monolithic, public mechanisms, generated by advertising and publicity. The most intimate desires of Westerners (she felt contemptuously) were echoes of slogans, catchphrases, and clichés. West Berlin youth, accustomed to a multiplicity of ready-made versions of truth, a veracity reducible to simple jingles, could not readily see behind official, manifest meanings.

Not only the methods but the motives for learning were different in West Berlin. In East Berlin, the difference in status and importance between college-bound students who went on to take the *Abitur* and those who quit after the tenth grade was insignificant. They frequented the same cafés, dances, and rock concerts and all belonged to the same official club, the FDJ (Free German Youth). In the "worker and farmer state," moreover, an egalitarian ideology served if anything to exalt future factory workers over future doctors. The most important social distinction was between students who became party members and those who did not, a distinction imposed by the authorities and not widely respected by the students. In West Berlin, by contrast, both the class origin of students and their apparent career goals were the basis for rigid hierarchical distinctions drawn by the students.

In the East the citizen's life course had in effect been planned by the state, regulated, and rendered predictable. The rules were codified and generally understood. Even the unwritten codicils to the state's expectations were well known, indeed a favorite topic of conversation. The citizen responded to the state as a reader to a text, accepting or ironizing, parodying, mocking its dictates. The master narrative of the individual life, however, was the state's exclusive production.

The school thus either earmarked the student for university study or it did not, and in a relatively uniform society it made little difference. The rewards for formal success were less substantial. Rising through the *Kader* system to become a party bureaucrat, for example, brought one very few privileges and placed one under direct ideological pressure to think and act correctly. Until the 1970s, moreover, pay scales in East Germany had remained relatively nonhierarchical. Even as late as 1986, a doctor such as Beate earned 1,500 marks a month, compared to an average wage for GDR workers of about 1,000 marks. If money was the goal, the way to earn it was often in nonprestigious jobs. Among my own acquaintances, the wealthiest with the shortest workdays were a doorman at a disco, a free-lance actor, a window washer, and an organizer of circuses.

Not accustomed to thinking of career incentives in terms of earned income, Franziska, while living in the East, had thought of becoming a potter or a graphic artist, anything where she could have some independence and be creative. Money was beside the point. Her future was secure regardless of what she earned. In the West her peers were all frenetically intent on becoming professionals. The degree to which their life courses were left open, a matter for their own manipulation and decision, seemed to subject them to outside influences and desires. Their ambitions were completely colonized by social models and they patterned their futures after preestablished trajectories toward wealth and status, surrendering their imaginations in an ecstasy of imitation and self-abnegation. In the East one could at least enter into a sort of dialogue with the prefabricated, master life narrative laid down for one by the state. One could talk back, imagine fantastic alternatives, ironize, mock. In the West there was no space for response, because the master narratives were internalized, inhabiting the fantasy lives and infecting the most private expressions of the unwitting citizenry. There were no written rules, only introjected patterns. Domination existed within the subject.

In the West, Franziska felt tracked implicitly toward university study by the circumstances of her mother's career and class status. She had no corresponding inner motivation, however, lacking the internalized dream, what in West Germany is called the *Ellenbogen* (elbowing) mentality. Beate fought for two years to get her daughter to take her grades seriously, but Theresa had no strong desire to get ahead. Yet, at heart, she could see no alternative. She accepted the patterns established for her by West German society but she could not feel at home in them, could not inhabit them emotionally.

She relied on her old friends in East Berlin, visiting them often, so often that Beate felt vaguely worried and resentful, particularly after her own visitation rights were abruptly revoked in 1988. Franziska went back almost daily, flaunting her ability to move freely across the Wall-scarred city.

This was perhaps the only thing she enjoyed, the freedom her inner homelessness allowed her. She could move between two cultures, two worlds, without having to belong to either.

The dismantling of the Wall again changed their routines. Franziska found it hard to shop because the stores were always full of East Germans. The crowds on the buses and subways, the hordes streaming down the sidewalks, made it difficult to move easily. The way back to her old stomping ground was mobbed. There was something else, however, something more ominous, something she didn't like about her reaction. It was the realization that she saw these people as foreigners. They were outsiders, invading a city that against her better judgment she saw as *hers*, thronging into a place she had adopted or that had expropriated her. They weren't her people anymore. They were the Other.

Beate confirmed this uneasy sense. "One of my first thoughts was, here they all come. It was wonderful, of course, but I also experienced it as a threat. I thought, what will we do?"

Who is the *we* here, the West or the East Berliners? Even Beate couldn't be sure. It was a pronoun without an antecedent, an unreal word. There was no clear *we* for either Beate or Franziska any longer. Franziska, most acutely, lived in a liminal land of perpetual, accepted alienation. She conformed to the expectations of her West German teachers, learned to fulfill their intricate demands and cut herself off from East German norms and models. Yet she did so without gusto or conviction. All her expectations came from without; inside she no longer seemed to look forward to anything. The moments she most enjoyed were ones of pure self-forgetfulness, parties, drinking, dancing.

The week when History came to town was, after all, great fun, but then, so were most weeks, more or less, less or more.

CUTTING AN ETHNIC GORDIAN KNOT

With the mass influx of refugees in 1989 and with the subsequent opening of the Wall, West Germany found a huge floating population on its hands, people who were "about to be" German. Thousands in resettlement camps had to be integrated into West German life. Millions were waiting in a disintegrating East Germany, anticipating their acceptance into a unified *Grossdeutschland,* the outlines of which were still unclear. The very nature of Germanness was in question everywhere, as the national identity was stretched to the limits of elasticity to accommodate these varying and intense demands.

The sheer administrative chaos was a nightmare for all concerned. The temptations for East Germans to rechristen themselves as West Germans by any means possible were enormous, and only increased when the Wall fell. Many pensioners and students found ways to establish a West Berlin residence and thus collect welfare benefits of some sort. GDR pensioners, for example, could collect a minimum of 470 Eastmarks monthly if they stayed at home. If they moved West and took advantage of their automatic West German citizenship, they could collect at least 1,600 deutschmarks. Converting back at the (low) rate of one to seven gave them a pension twenty times what they could have had in the East. Meanwhile, students from East Germany, who have the right as "Germans" to study in any West German university, could collect a West German grant of 850 deutschmarks per month. When this was exchanged at the one-to-seven rate, they acquired more money than the Prime Minister of the GDR.

When GDR citizens resettle in the West, they normally apply for special benefits. Many take particular advantage of a law permitting them to be "written sick" for a period of six months to a year. A study of such resettlers in the first six months of 1989 found that over 60 percent took this sick pay, claiming such illnesses as "resettler's syndrome" and "adaptation difficulties." The open border has strained the West German medical system. East Germans have the right to free emergency treatment in the West; in practice this has come to include nearly everything in short supply in the East, from expensive operations to new eyeglasses.

From the very inception of the West German state, its promise of full membership in the FRG polity to any immigrating German has compelled it to codify Jesuitical definitions of what Germanness entails. Eleven to fifteen categories (the lists vary according to circumstances) distinguish the degrees of Germanness and hence the responsibilities of the state toward the petitioner for citizenship. Under the stresses of impending reunification, this system of distinctions is nearing collapse. Numerous nonethnic Germans have also staked claims on the resources of the state. Poles have presented a particularly thorny problem, intensified by German responsibilities unconfronted since the Second World War, for West Germany never signed a peace treaty with or paid reparations to Poland.

According to Paragraph 6 of the Refugee Law, Poles can apply to resettle if they can prove they are known as German in their homeland. The vast majority of Poles today are appealing under what is called Category 3 of the German *Volksgruppe.* During the war the Nazis compiled lists of Slavs who had no German blood but were considered capable of racial integration into a Germanized Europe— who were *eindeutschungsfähig.* Up to 1.7 million people may qualify as descendants of these elect few.

The next most common basis for appeal is documentation of descent from a Nazi soldier. The relationships of domination and humiliation encoded in these bureaucratic niceties, in which access to German identity and German wealth can be gained, for example, by proving one's grandmother was raped by the SS, can be left to the imagination. Despite the obstacles, in 1988 and 1989, 370,000 Poles applied as *Aussiedler* to resettle in the Federal Republic.

The reworking of German identity is thus a complex and many-faceted problem, a Gordian knot woven of steel wire. Perhaps the most acute, if not the most overt, difficulty the new German state will face lies within the troubled subjectivity of the East Germans it wishes to absorb. Many of these potential citizens are paralyzed by an anomie separating them drastically from both the state that reared them and the state that claims them. They seem victims of an ambivalence both historically specific and almost paradigmatically modern.

Good burghers though they may be, they call to mind the evocations of exile running through twentieth-century art and literature, the visions of modernity as an age in which the self is homeless, "a wanderer between two worlds," as Matthew Arnold wrote, "one dead, the other powerless to be born." East Germans such as Klaus, Marianne, and Franziska are literally caught between two worlds, their ability to narrate and comprehend themselves thwarted by the divisions in their own histories. A newly articulated German identity that hopes to include them must acknowledge these very real scars. Any version of German selfhood which does not do so will only create further divisions, pitting its abstract and streamlined ideal of history against the truth of human lives.

10

The Election and the End of the Revolution

This is the time for the tellable!
Here is its country!
—Rainer Maria Rilke, *Duino Elegy IX*

WITH A FREE VOTE YOU GET HOOPLA

On Sunday, 18 March 1990, East Germans held the first
free election on their territory since 1933—the first fully
free election in Eastern Europe since the Second World
War. For most citizens it was their first experience with
the secret ballot. On that afternoon, I sat with Arnim outside the Communist party headquarters, a building that
had been the symbol of the obsessive secretiveness of the
leadership through the years of SED rule.

"This building is like the White House to me," explained Arnim. "You don't understand what it's like to go inside. Imagine if you could just on your own go around inside the White House. It's an incredible feeling."

The building was filled with people of all ages. Free lunches had been passed out and open discussions went on in all the rooms. That evening, party leaders Gregor Gysi and Hans Modrow sat on a dais and answered the questions of a gathering in the large assembly hall.

Meanwhile, across the street in Karl Marx Platz, the world's broadcasting systems had taken over the Palace of the Republic for their election coverage. A cordon of police was assigned to keep the people at bay. Only media figures and politicians were allowed into this new inner sanctum of power. Nothing could more clearly embody the significance of the election, the transfer of power about to occur. The brief interregnum of confusion was about to end. The old regime was enforced by guns; in the regime to come, images would rule. As before, however, the closer one came to "the people," the further one would be from the real heart of power.

Ninety-two percent of the voting-age population went to the polls to choose among twenty-four parties. Over 48 percent supported the conservative coalition of three parties (Christian Democratic Union [CDU], Democratic Awakening [DA], and German Social Union [DSU]) which called itself the Alliance for Germany. The Social Democratic party (SPD), heavily favored only weeks before, won a mere 21 percent of the vote. The restructured Communist party, newly named the party of Democratic Socialism (PDS), surprised many with a showing of 16 percent. Bündnis '90, a loose union of left-alternative groups (New Forum [NF], Democracy Now [DJ], and Initiative for Peace and Human

Rights [IFN])—groups that started the revolutionary process—won the support of 2.9 percent of the people.

On election day Alexander Platz hummed with activity. Two well-scrubbed young men with slicked-back hair passed out free Stuyvesant cigarettes. The slogan "Come Together" was emblazoned on their T-shirts. Already reunification had become a sales pitch.

During most of the afternoon the main stage erected on Alex was occupied by a hard-rock group from the United States, with long, straggly hair and torn jeans, resting their screeching guitars on their genitals. People watched in stunned silence. After one song the lead guitarist ululated (in English, of course): "Hello East Germany! How you doing?"

About fifty feet from the stage, right next to the World Clock, stood a grotesquely overgrown Coca Cola can, about eight feet tall and five feet wide, a plasticine, pituitary monstrosity from which someone was selling cola.

INTERVENTION AND AN OPPORTUNITY MISSED

One popular explanation for the election results was that *Nur Kohl bringt die Kohle*: "Only Kohl will bring us the cabbage/money." Or did they mean cola? The real winner of the election was not an East German but the well fed greengrocer-to-all-the-Germans Helmut Kohl, Chancellor of the Federal Republic. In this atmosphere of a veritable cargo cult, the promise of delivering the goods, whether deutschmarks, cabbage, or Coca-Kohla, led him and his allies to victory.

His Christian Democratic party and its Bavarian partner (the Christian Social Union [CSU]) had pumped 4.5 million deutschmarks ($2.7 million) into the campaign. The other major West German parties, Kohl's other coalition partner the Free Democrats (FDP) and the opposition Social Democrats (SPD), had each invested a total of 1.5 million deutschmarks ($880,000) in their East German sister parties. The East German round table, a group representing all social interests set up at the height of the Autumn Revolution to monitor and control the democratization process, had voted to ban election intervention by foreign states and political parties. Only the West German Green party tried to respect the resolution, much to their detriment. The East German Greens (in an alliance with the Independent Women's Association) won less than 2 percent of the vote.

In the two months before the election the five largest West German political parties organized 205 campaign rallies. Kohl's CDU organized 74 and his Bavarian partners 20; the SPD 60; the FDP 48; and the Greens 3. East Germans, unused to sophisticated media campaigns, were awed by the efficient West German organizations, by their professional, well paid staffs, prodigious technical capacities, and ability to "spin" the news. Several people told me, "If Kohl can bring overnight so much money and equipment and organizational ability, then he's the one most likely to deliver the goods quickly and efficiently after the election."

Kohl campaigned vigorously for his own party. Gregor Gysi, the chair of the Communist party, joked at a rally two days before the election that "The Chancellor has been spending so much time with us lately that perhaps they don't need him in West Germany anymore! Well," Gysi added, "we don't need him either."

The strategy of supporting East German counterparts paid off for the major parties, but the question lingers: Under what conditions does a foreign state have the right to interfere in the election process of another state? Surely the juridical formality of East German independence should have stood for something. An election is an act of legitimation, an affirmation of precisely the legal principles of sovereignty and self-rule so conspicuously flouted in the East German campaign. West German political parties did not even bother shrouding their intervention under the pretense of guaranteeing a "free election." They openly intended to influence the election results. What if France or the Soviet Union had poured in 7.5 million deutschmarks to support (or even create) parties favoring their explicit national goals? Do we judge the fairness of such intervention merely on the basis of who the intervening power may be?

"We want to be *dick, fett, und satt*" (thick, fat, and full) was how most opposition leaders accounted for their compatriots' desire for Kohl. Many added that their fellow East Germans, knowing Kohl controlled the purse strings on West German investment, voted for him from purely tactical motives. Others felt Kohl triumphed as the best known alternative, that East Germans, nauseated by their recent roller coaster ride, wanted stability and stolidity, not further experiment. All these commentators were probably right. What the election signified above all, beyond the election's winners and losers, was the end of the revolution begun with the mass flights and mass protests of autumn 1989. The revolution, started as a struggle to revitalize socialism by making it more democratic, culminated in the abolition of socialism and the triumph of consumer culture. East Germany would dissolve as a state, West Germany would annex its territory, and the people within this territory would be expected to take on the same social structure—laws, class structure, inner identity—as the West Germans.

It was the last choice offered East Germans about their own identity. Henceforth they will find themselves voting at ritual intervals, but the vote will not enable them to change radically the power structures of their society. The opportunity for an *Umgestaltung*, reconfiguration, has passed. Future elections on the onetime soil of East Germany will be elaborately staged public spectacles, with the concomitant politicians, media, polling experts, and election analysts all there to legitimate the voting and affirm that it was conducted according to the rules. The rules will be fixed. The ritually legitimated elections will merely offer a ritual legitimation of capitalist, liberal-democratic systems of hegemony. They will offer no opportunity to change the political structure. At most they will change the names that flesh out that structure, and shuffle around component parts from slot to slot.

THE POLITICAL LINEUP

The leading candidates of the various parties in East Germany were not uniformly the sorts of politicians their West German supporters would have preferred, although they and their campaign staffs were tailored and trained to dress and act much like their ideological counterparts in the West. Ironically—or perhaps fittingly—the leaders of two of the three parties in the conservative Alliance for Germany had good connections with the old Communist leadership. Lothar de Maiziere, a lawyer known for defending young men who refused to do military service, had been second in command of the East German Christian Democratic party (CDU), one of the bloc parties that had long cooperated with the ruling Communists in the Socialist Unity party (SED). De Maiziere did not have a reputation as a dissident, and played no role in the Autumn Revolution of 1989. He is a small, thin man (about half the size of Kohl) with a trimmed beard. His untelegenically crooked teeth occasion constant comment. His campaign slogans were "Never Again Socialism," "No Experiment," and "Freedom and Prosperity."

The German Social Union, sister party to the Bavarian Christian Democrats, was led by the Reverend Hans-Wilhelm Ebeling of Leipzig. Ebeling was best known for his church's famous boys' choir. Many men of the cloth had actively supported the opposition before and during the revolution, but Reverend Ebeling was not one of them. On 8 October 1989 in Leipzig, immediately after Gorbachev's visit, the state security had begun planning its "China Solution," to open fire on all demonstrators. All the churches in Leipzig and in Berlin opened their doors to give refuge to the demonstrators that Monday night— except one, Reverend Ebeling's. Nonetheless (or perhaps precisely because of this) he received over 6 percent of the vote in a late-starting but well financed campaign. Ebeling, more than all other candidates, appealed to German nationalist sentiments tinged with xenophobia.

The third member of the Alliance, Democratic Awakening, was led, in the final days before the election, by the Reverend Rainer Eppelmann. Four days before the vote, the leader of the party, Wolfgang Schnur, suffering from exhaustion and confined to a hospital bed, admitted he had been an agent for the Stasi. Eppelmann took over at the last minute, burdened by the newfound ironies in the DA campaign slogan, "The Honest Alternative." He managed

less than 1 percent of the vote, but will play a disproportionate role in the government. His party's stance, slightly
to the left of other members of the Alliance, qualifies it as
a bridge between centrist and leftist groups, a corrective
for ideological differences in the governing coalition.

The Social Democrats were led by Ibrahim Böhme, who
had spent fifteen months in prison for his opposition activities. Abandoned by his mother, his father and his birthdate
unknown, raised in an orphanage, Böhme stood above all
for social justice and a "thoughtful integration" into the
Federal Republic—too thoughtful for most of his compatriots. Much like many of his generation's West German
counterparts, he appeared young and articulate, but col-
orless. He ran under the nondescript slogan "A Better Future." Shortly after the election, Böhme came under
suspicion for having cooperated with the Stasi and was
forced to resign as party leader.

The restructured Communist party was led by Gregor
Gysi, but its most attractive candidate was the taciturn and
well respected Prime Minister Hans Modrow. Having lost
or expelled nearly two-thirds of its members, the party pro-
fessed itself purged and streamlined. It campaigned aggressively, but could not overcome its history or profound
popular mistrust. Still, it succeeded in rejuvenating itself
as a credible opposition, a party of democratic socialism,
no longer intent on ruling but determined to stand for certain principles. Gysi consistently said he looked forward to
working in the opposition, and in fact felt most comfortable there. Reportedly three-fourths of those who supported the PDS were never members of the Communist
party. Like all other major parties, the PDS supported German unification, but argued that it should be carried
forward slowly, with protection for the social policy

achievements of the past. Unlike the other major parties, the PDS supported demilitarization and elimination of standing armies in both states. (The SPD had initially held such a position; after joining forces with their West German counterparts, however, they were persuaded to back away.)

Gysi, whose Jewish father hid underground during the war, had a comparatively untainted reputation. In the past he had defended the regime's most prominent opponents, including the painter Bärbel Bohley, the economist Rudolf Bahro, and the physicist Robert Havemann. He was one of the leaders in organizing the huge November Fourth demonstration in Berlin that catalyzed the final collapse of the regime. Gysi campaigned with irreverent humor, breathing life into a political corpse that would be impossible to resuscitate in the other Eastern European countries. "A Strong Opposition for the Weak" and "Don't Worry, Take Gysi!"—a play on the American jingle "Don't Worry, Take It Easy"—were two of his major election slogans.

One of the PDS's most effective campaign posters showed an *Arschkriecher*, literally, someone who crawls into an ass, what in English we would call a brownnose. The poster showed the West German insignia branded on a flabby pair of buttocks, and a man's legs sticking from between them. A ladder leans against the rump and a line of men waits below to climb in. Under the *Arschkriecher* is the caption, *Der Anschluss ist besetzt*, "The connection is already occupied." This plays on both the resonant idea of political *Anschluss* or annexation, and a telephone operator's typical response when a line is busy. (Telephone lines connecting the two Germanies were in many cases severed by the GDR after building the Wall, making it extremely difficult to telephone from East to West.) The East Germans, the poster intimates, are brownnoses, lining up to be absorbed by West Germany through its asshole.

A West German cartoon, published in *Der Spiegel* two weeks after the election, presented this anal-retentive vision in even more repulsive terms. West Germans, after all, feared not absorption but being asked to give, and give, and give. The cartoon showed Kohl and de Maiziere's different daydreams about the meaning of the election. In Kohl's dream, the ponderous triple-chinned chancellor rides the tiny ass, de Maiziere, toward victory in the December 1990 West German elections. In de Maiziere's dream, the bespectacled, recessive East German sits backward atop the colossal upturned rump of a stationary Kohl, holding Kohl's tail up so that deutschmarks can pour out of the rear into a pail marked with a GDR symbol. In the cartoon, both partners are happy with the arrangements.

One factor which played only a minimal role in this election, but may affect future ones, is gender. The Independent Women's Association, in an alliance with the Green party, received less than 2 percent of the vote, partly, perhaps, because of the hands-off attitude of the West German Green party. The Greens and feminists' future need not be so dismal as the tallies suggest, however. In many ways, eventual unification will affect women more drastically than men. GDR women have much to lose if the West German legal system is taken over without safeguarding the protections and social programs accorded them under socialism, such as child-care subsidies, free abortions, "affirmative action" programs, and programs to alleviate the double burden of work and house care for working mothers. Women also occupy more than 60 percent of the positions in the bureaucracy, an area likely to be cut severely in the next several years. Hence women may have incentives to organize politically on a scale uncommon even in the West.

THE CITY IS LEFT

In this election, the city of Berlin showed itself to be something of an anomaly. There the conservative Alliance won only 21 percent of the vote, while the SPD received 35 percent. The restructured Communists in the PDS won 30, and the Bündnis '90 garnered 6.4 percent. The left side of the political spectrum in Berlin won over 70 percent of the vote.

Some of the support for the PDS can be explained by the numbers of civil servants and government employees in Berlin, a status-quo-centered group of voters clinging to the PDS because they had nowhere else to turn. There are two other factors, however, setting East Berlin apart from the rest of the republic. First, its proximity to West Berlin, currently ruled by a coalition of the SPD and Green party, has meant more exposure to the West in general and to other critical European intellectuals in particular. Its images of the West were more long-standing and wide-ranging, and more questioning, than the TV pictures devoured by the rest of the country. Second, the old regime had favored Berlin in renovation, construction, and consumer goods. Berliners had it much better than others in the GDR and they did not feel the urgency of reform as did workers in Suhl or Karl-Marx-Stadt or Leipzig or Halle, where the air stinks and the water is poisoned, where the buildings are collapsing and the industries are producing at a great loss.

FREEDOM AT LAST! OR IS IT?

Reactions to the election ranged from euphoria to anguish. Bärbel Bohley, longtime dissident and cofounder of New Forum, sobbed so uncontrollably on hearing the results that the media determined her unfit to be interviewed. For Bohley, as for other former dissidents and leaders of the pro-democracy and proenvironmental movements, the victory of the conservative forces meant a loss of sovereignty. It meant the end of a short democratic experiment and an exchange of grass roots democracy for material well-being. Surveillance of East German activists by the despised and now disbanded state security would likely be replaced with surveillance by the West German Office of Constitutional Protection, certainly less crude and powerful than the East German Stasi, but nonetheless omnipresent for members of the German left, and often amazingly effective in blocking their access to jobs.

At a party on the eve of the election, I was sitting at a table with some friends. On my right was the mother of one of the hosts, a sixty-four-year-old woman named Vera who was going to vote Christian Democratic. She and her husband had volunteered to work at their neighborhood polling place the next day. Under the old regime elections had been organized by party hacks. This election was the responsibility of the Round Table, but few people were willing to work in setting up the election machinery. Vera had enthusiastically stepped into this void, but she had no idea what to do. They would have to train her the next morning in the hour before the polls opened.

"Freedom," Vera gushed, addressing all of us at the table. "Freedom! I wake up each morning with freedom on my mind. I am so happy to finally be free, to live for this day when I can finally vote, express my opinions freely without worrying what the neighbor thinks. I had it out with my neighbor last week—one of those who stood on the other side—and told him exactly what I thought. And we still greet each other on the street. He's much friendlier to me now.

"Finally, after forty-five years of dictatorship, not counting the years under Hitler. The Communists have no right to rule anymore—no rights at all, for anything. They've ruined everything in this country. What have we worked for all these years?

"No, freedom!" she repeated in a kind of ritual chant, changing the verse but securely returning to the refrain. "Freedom! I can finally say what I think! I can express my opinions without fear. That is freedom for me."

The man on my left whispered to me, "She used to say the same thing before. Her problem is that she has no opinions of her own to express."

I asked her whether the coming adjustments under capitalism worried her. "No," she replied emphatically. "None of my friends in West Germany sleeps under a bridge. They all have homes, they all take vacations to Italy and France.

"I want to be able to pick out a dress that I want. Whenever I visit my friends in the West, who are all well dressed, I have to wear whatever I could find here to buy. Never have I been able to buy what I wanted. At last, I want to buy something that fits my tastes, exactly what I want. Is that so bad of me? My whole life I've dressed worse than they did. I've always had to pick from what was available, never what I wanted. Just once in my life. Then I'll be satisfied. Yes, Freedom! I'm so happy to experience this. You can't imagine what this means to me. I never thought I'd live to see the day."

I asked why, if life was so bad in the German Democratic Republic, she hadn't left for West Germany.

"We did," she explained quietly. "That was 1953. You see, my husband was involved in the worker uprising back then. He was very active politically at his job, active in the party, too, and we feared he would be arrested. But we couldn't find work in West Berlin. Our friends there couldn't find an apartment for us. We were living in a refugee camp, and I had my two sons to take care of. At the end of two months we were all sick. My father-in-law arranged for us to come back. He said we could get our old apartment back, and my husband could get his job back, and we wouldn't be penalized. We had no choice. Back then, women followed their husbands. Today, I wouldn't do it. I'd tell him, 'You go if you like.' But back then, we didn't stand up for ourselves."

A married man in his early fifties named Peter, sitting to Vera's right, mustered his nerve to contradict her. Peter sits on the board of a local parish; he has been active in promoting tolerance for minorities.

"I don't think you Americans will like to hear this," he said, directing his remarks to me, "but I don't think too highly of liberal democracy. It won't bring us very much."

"No!" Vera interrupted him abruptly. "It's freedom we have now. I'm really looking forward to voting. To live in freedom. To be able to express my mind."

"I don't agree," Peter continued. "My life hasn't been all bad here. Besides, it doesn't make much difference for whom you vote. They'll do with us whatever they want. I've worked hard for what tolerance there is in my church, and I think we've accomplished a great deal."

Vera's husband broke in, "But we haven't been able to

vote for forty-five years. Now, finally we have the chance we were never given."

"That's no reason to vote," snapped Peter, "just because you haven't done it for five decades."

"You're right," Vera corrected herself. "Life hasn't been all bad here. And you have done a lot for minorities here. The important thing is, after the election, that they form a coalition government, the Social and Christian Democrats. Just not the Communists. I'm sorry. Excuse me. I get so excited about this. I just can't help it. I'm finally free to say what I want."

Vera's son then entered the room, and Peter took his arrival as an excuse to leave us. "John and I have been engaged in a conversation," Vera told her son. She turned to me. "We had a good discussion, didn't we?"

STILL IN CHARGE

Helmut's wife, Marina, who voted for the Greens, was sick, flat in bed, for the entire week after the election. Helmut told me she was in agony. She had been a member of the Communist party until the end of January. I talked to her later in the week, when she had just returned from a parent-teacher meeting.

"Things haven't changed," she said despairingly. "We have the same principal at the school. She's no longer a member of the Communist party—those were the first people to drop out—and she now uses all the right words. First she lectured us about democracy, how we had to listen to parents' wishes and teachers should use their own initiative. And as soon as parents suggested any changes or the reading teacher asked if she might create separate groups for advanced readers and slow readers, the principal responded, 'Oh, no! We have to wait for the new laws. Each school can't make up its own rules.' The same old thing. The same people who controlled before have the leading positions, but now they're all 'democrats.' "

Helmut voted for the Independent Women's Association, which ran in a coalition with the Green party. He wanted to make sure women's interests were represented in the new parliament. Their son Jonah was extremely disappointed that he couldn't vote. Everyone else was doing it, the TV made it sound like Lindt chocolate, why was he left out? Only when they both assured him that they would vote for the Greens' coalition was he somewhat placated.

Since he came of age in 1970, Helmut had always cast the same vote: "no." The ballots of the old regime listed ten individuals, with no mention of what political party or interests they represented. One could vote "yes" for all of them, as over 98 percent of voters did, by folding the ballot in two and putting it in the ballot box. One thus passed through the line without ever entering a voting booth. In order to vote "no," one had to go into the booth and with pencil or pen, strike the name of the candidates one opposed. Election officials made note of those few who entered the booth; their names were turned over to the Stasi.

Helmut had even heard stories of election workers going into nursing homes to record the votes of the elderly. Many patients there not only couldn't remember the candidates, but had forgotten their own names. The election workers would take the ballot to each person and fold it for them before sticking it into the ballot box.

In municipal elections in May 1989, opposition groups had organized a protest vote. West German television informed people in the GDR how to vote "no.": take a pencil along, clearly strike out the full name, fold the ballot only once, etc. The opposition groups sent observers to polling places to estimate how many entered the booths. Predictably, the official results, which recorded over 98 percent of voters as having cast an automatic "yes," deviated radically from the opposition's figures. This open falsification of results, which severely wounded the regime's credibility, was supervised by the good apparatchik Egon Krenz—one major reason he was never accepted as a legitimate alternative to Honecker.

SUPPORTING THE PEOPLE

In mid-February, Hildegard decided to join the new Social Democratic party. She consulted neither husband, family, nor friends. "I decided it was important I do something, make the decision for myself for real personal reasons, and support the new Social Democrats here."

I asked her which politicians she liked. She found Gysi lacking in humanity. "That's often the case with short men [Gysi is about 5 feet, 4 inches in height]; they have to project themselves larger than they are. He is not a man who can be the father of a nation."

"Who is such a man for you?" I asked.

"Helmut Schmidt. Weizäcker. Willy Brandt. I think Helmut Schmidt is a great man because he can sit down at the piano and play. He doesn't have to make himself greater than he is, because he has enough inside of himself to rely on his own strengths."

Before the election, her father sent her a letter explaining why she and Bert should vote for the Christian Democrats. She sent back a sharply worded reply, rebuking him for supporting a party that offered only money from the West and nothing of its own. Bert ended up voting for Bündnis '90; he wanted to support the people in New Forum. A cousin of his who had worked for years on citizen initiatives and in environmental groups complained to Bert that nobody would listen to his kind anymore. Bert said, "We owed it to them. They should be sitting in the parliament also."

"WE'RE STAYING . . ."

Arnim voted for the Social Democrats. "I couldn't vote for the Communists. They're like a corpse now. And I couldn't vote for the Christian Democrats; my friends would kill me."

After Arnim and I heard the election count, a young man with his preadolescent son asked us if we knew who had won. We told him the CDU and their Alliance might well have won an absolute majority. He looked overjoyed and said, "Oliver, we're staying after all."

"That explains it," Arnim observes. "There's why. They're all sitting on packed suitcases, and now they think they can all make their fortunes as entrepreneurs, so they'll stay here and give capitalism a try."

THE UNREGENERATE RADICAL

Regine and all her family and friends voted for the PDS. She said the other parties were too bourgeois for her, and only the opposition groups and the PDS weren't already bought out by West German interests. She wanted the interests of the GDR represented and saw only the PDS capable of asserting them. She knew the PDS would be left in opposition, but she was satisfied with that, fearing a civil war if they actually won. She liked the small left parties, but did not think they had enough strength or experience to be effective.

She thought the renewal of the party had been effective if incomplete. "You can't just kick out all the old dogmatists," she said. "They also have to be incorporated somehow. But when I went to several PDS meetings, I did feel myself with people I was sympathetic to. The older members have a great burden to carry, and they should be made responsible and conscious of this, not simply kicked out."

Regine's concern for remembering, and for reintegrating the past, even at its most disturbing, with the chaotic present, is perhaps particularly informed by her own work situation. Her job as a documentarist at DEFA will probably be eliminated in a labor-rationalization effort when the film studio is bought and reorganized by a West German firm. Her friends advised her to join a new project, financed and organized by West Berliners, to make a documentary on the history of the German Democratic Republic.

The Westerners wanted an East German familiar with the material at hand. Regine soon found herself in a deeply troubling position.

"I'm being forced to engage in historical falsification," she told me. "I never had to do this before, and yet today here I am, my hand is forced. I told them there were certain things I wouldn't do, and they said they understood my political sentiments and were not interested in portraying the history of the last forty years one-sidedly. But I know they are going to falsify it."

I asked how she knew this.

"In how they select materials," she said. "They choose certain pictures and not others, in order to show the history of East Germany has been all negative. But what can I do? I have no choice. We don't know what will happen to our apartments, how much the rent will increase, who will control the lease. With this job I think I can manage. That's the only reason I've taken it on."

TOLERANCE IN OPPOSITION

Frau Gruner told me that the women in her sauna asked her whom they should vote for. A female friend from Leipzig, a medical doctor, even wrote asking for advice.

" 'It should be a secret vote,' I told them. 'I'm voting for the PDS,' I said, and I explained why. 'You should decide for yourself.' " Two of her daughters also voted for the reorganized Communists in the PDS. The third, who, with her husband had been one of the founders of New Forum, voted for Bündnis '90.

Why did she vote for the PDS? "It is extremely important that we have a strong opposition on the left. The SPD will do the same things as the CDU if they have power. The PDS is also offering *Realpolitik* today, not just ideology or fantasy, and I like that.

"I am particularly taken," she added, "by their campaign methods and by their confrontation with the past. They are honest about the Stalinist past, not trying to sweep it under the rug. And in the campaign, Herr Gysi was marvelous. He was a student of mine, you know. Back then he wasn't very interested in family law, I could tell. Once I was discussing a particular problem, and thought I should perhaps call on Herr Gysi to see what he thinks about this. He had been doing something else; I could tell his attention was elsewhere. So he asked, 'Would you please repeat the question?' The students laughed. But he had something interesting to say once he understood the question. He just didn't take family law that seriously.

"I think Gysi has been successful in cleaning up the party. I can only speak about the party in the district where I live. The base has changed, and that has been brought about by young, intelligent people, not imposed from the top down. And I hear that is also the case in the party in other districts. In the University, leadership of the party by younger comrades is supposedly still quite limited. The students' hearts are elsewhere. But overall, young people have moved into the party and forced changes.

"I am now busy with a group of men who are trying to get visiting rights to their children, something that is written in the constitution but has never been enforced. Over ninety-five percent of the time, the mother receives the children after a divorce, and that is not what the law says. I helped write that law. Both parents are to have equal rights, and the court must decide in the interests of the child. But instead, they have tried to placate the mothers, who then take the children and deny the father visiting rights. They do this because there are no punitive sanctions when they refuse. I've written petitions to the Central Committee, the constitutional court, and the parliament. They all refused to answer.

"A group of fathers in Leipzig who had been denied access to their children began organizing, and contacted me to see if I would help them. Now we have contact with similar groups in West Germany, and I think something will come of this. We are basing our appeals on a United

Nations declaration concerning the rights of children. I see our function as informing the public about what the situation is."

Then she added, reflectively, "Many partnerships do not have to end in divorce, if only there were more tolerance for one another. It is easier simply to quit speaking with one another. People here haven't learned to communicate, haven't learned democracy. That is the answer."

OUT OF THE FRYING PAN?

Perhaps, too, that is the only answer this book can provide and the seeming banality of the weighty, all-purpose word *democracy*! is a measure of our collective dilemma.

The future of the two Germanies now becoming one encompasses uncertainty, absurdity, and foregone conclusions. Among the latter may be counted the inevitability of reunification itself. Other questions, such as the fate of the social benefits provided under the East German system, of individual East Germans during the difficult transition period, and of Helmut Kohl himself in his contests with Social Democrats and Greens before and after unification, are murkier. So, too, are the precise stakes that NATO and the Soviet Union will retain in the Germany they occupied and divided for 45 years. Each successive day seems to make the shape of the post-Cold War world less predictable, less clear.

The scope of this book has been narrow. I have tried to describe the nature of a vanishing society. Circumscribed by those limits, I can say one thing with certainty, that "actually existing socialism," socialism as it was established in Eastern Europe after the war, is extinct in East Germany. Nor is it likely to be revived in the foreseeable future. Few leftists looking at its limited accomplishments and its extensive failures, at the lives warped and the productive capacities stunted, at the regime of fear and want and recuperative fantasy imposed upon the people, can afford to mourn it for very long.

It would, however, be presumptuous and premature to claim that true democracy has succeeded socialism. Rather, severe material, economic, and financial constraints have succeeded overt political control in creating a regime of fear that governs and restricts the choices of the East Germans. The flight to capitalism has not been democratically chosen, but rather imposed by a situation of radical uncertainty, rampant devaluation, and severe inequity.

Many East German intellectuals, especially those in New Forum and affiliated groups, blame the East Germans themselves for betraying the revolution. In their view, the population simply sold out, abandoning its ideals for bananas and better washing machines, giving up its (variously and vaguely defined) socialist birthright for a mess of publicity and pots and pans.

One should beware before accepting this easy explanation. There is nothing wrong—it seems absurdly necessary to emphasize—with wanting better goods, a better life, the elimination of drudgery and shortages, a choice of fruits and a decent potassium intake. There is nothing wrong with wanting comfort. A leftist perspective that ignores or denigrates the aspirations of the masses toward improved material conditions is untrue to its own materialism. In its arrogant condemnation of elemental desires, in its willingness to sacrifice the dream of lessened labor and diminished pain for the sake of a backhandedly spiritualized Spartan ideal, it unwittingly exposes what Stanley Aronowitz calls the "puritanical political unconscious" of much modern leftist thought. Such thought "offers the Protestant ethic in revolutionary garb" as its only and singularly unattractive response to capitalist ideology.[1]

Socialism failed, in its 45-year history, to deliver the goods. A combination of internal inadequacies and the external disadvantage of the proximity of a hostile capitalist power contributed to this failure, circumstances that will no doubt be exhaustively analyzed by future historians. It is enough now to observe that capitalism succeeded in promoting a utopian vision of abundance which actually existing socialism could only adumbrate in its ideologizing.

There is one inescapable caveat. Capitalism brought abundance at a price. In a system of universal fungibility, freedom from want is subject to the principle of exchange. The price paid by East Germans in assimilating themselves into a capitalist society is the loss of opportunity for self-articulation: for democratic discourse, for free and full exchange of opinions among individuals and interest groups. Instead, they settled for a prolongation of the passivity learned under the socialist system, for the serene all-embracing receptivity of children learning phrases and political slogans by rote from the TV, for the stupefied indifference of shoppers led by the brand name and by the hand. The opportunity to claim their own words, their own voices, was buried under the onslaught of images and of a prefabricated language.

Perhaps the most pregnant question left by the difficult parturition of a united Germany is why the abundance that capitalism brings seems inevitably to be accompanied by the proportionate depoliticization and paralysis of its subjects. There is no law either of economics or psychology that dictates that a washing machine should stupefy social awareness or that a shopping bag full of fruit should evis-cerate the will to organize and vote. Yet in the exchange system of capitalist society, such barters of self-expression and self-will for the material objects of desire take place every day. It is not the desire of East Germans for con-sumer goods we should question. It is the malignant logic imposed on those goods themselves, making them synec-doches and substitutes for effective political action. It is the use of cars and canned food and cartons of milk, not to sate needs but to stun citizens into submission. It is the transformation of mere things into invisible truncheons, instruments to silence the multiplicity and complexity of human voices. It is the vast resignification of the object-world under the regime of modernity, transforming mute creation into a shelf of placebos. It is the mechanism be-hind this malign, almost magical transformation that, in the new era before us, deserves our intimate attention.

Neither socialism nor capitalism has achieved democ-racy. The failure of both systems to call upon the full hu-man potential for dignity and self-expression, to elicit the widest, freest range of voices from their dulled or stifled citizens, reminds us that, even in a century that has seen more advances in technology and productivity than any other, history remains at heart a story of waste. We waste ourselves, our capacity for language, for the meaningful speech that makes us human. Our wasted voices are our wasted lives. We vanish into the emptiness of unsaid things and the air will not record our passing.

The revolution was not without its lessons. The banners of 4 November perhaps preserve, in memory, a trace of the utopian dream of a truly democratic outpouring, a people coming together in the absence of preordained structures or established rules to constitute themselves as a people, to *say* themselves freely for the first time. Those banners do not vanish into silence. They linger in the mind. They provide both a rudimentary model and a real hope for popular, genuinely open speech.

Such moments are not the less powerful for being fleeting, for having been superannuated in the swift onrush of history. In an age where change is the only permanent condition, the secret of permanence may lie in pure evanescence. The brief and broken may contain the essence of the ephemeral whole. Facing a future where all is both ambiguous and seemingly already decided somewhere else, one might well say (as Brecht did at the end of *Jungle of Cities*, that terrifying play about freedom conceived as terror): "The chaos is gone. It was the best time. And now it is used up."

Notes

Chapter 1

1. For all statistics and direct citations of official personalities, I have relied, unless otherwise noted, on two sources, the Hamburg weekly *Der Spiegel* (issues 32–52, 1989, and 1–14, 1990) and *DDR Journal zur Novemberrevolution* (TAZ, December 1989, Berlin). Alternate possible sources of record, such as the East German daily newspaper *Neues Deutschland* or the West German weekly *Die Zeit,* have not varied significantly from the others in reporting the events, official speech, and statistics referred to in this book. Since most of the material was gathered firsthand, either by attending the events, seeing them, or hearing the participants directly, I have used newspapers and journals more to corroborate and verify than to cite as primary sources.

2. Sebastian Haffner, *Anmerkungen zur Hitler* (Munich: Kindler, 1978).

3. See Hermann Korte, "Bevökerungsstruktur und Entwicklung," in *Die Bundesrepublik Deutschland*, Band 2, ed. Wolfgang Benz (Frankfurt: Fischer, 1985); Wolfgang Meinicke, "Zur Integration der Umsiedler in die Gesellschaft 1945–1952," *Zeitschrift für Geschichstwissenschaft* 36, Heft 10, 1988.
4. Jacques Rupnik, "Central Europe or Mitteleuropa?" *Daedalus* 119:1, 1990.
5. Tony Judt, "The Rediscovery of Central Europe," *Daedalus* 119:1, 1990. For a more supportive view of the viability of a Central Europe, see the work of Timothy Garton Ash, *The Uses of Adversity* (New York: Random House, 1989).
6. Friederich Meinecke, *Cosmopolitanism and the National State*, trans. Robert B. Kimber (Princeton: Princeton University Press, 1970). See also the superb account of the role of the nation in Germany, from which some of this is drawn, by James J. Sheehan, "What is German History? Reflections on the Role of the Nation in German History and Historiography," *Journal of Modern History*, 53:1, 1981. Also see Werner Conze, " 'Deutschland' und 'deutsche Nation' als historische Begriffe," in *Die Rolle der Nation in der Deutschen Geschichte und Gegenwart*, eds. Otto Buesch and James J. Sheehan (Berlin: Colloquium, 1985), and George Mosse, *Toward the Final Solution: A History of European Racism* (Madison: University of Wisconsin, 1978).
7. Johann Gottfried Herder, "Ideen zur Philosophie der Geschichte der Menschheit," in *Sämmtliche Werke*, vol. 13, ed. Bernhard Suphan (Berlin, 1887).
8. Leopold von Ranke, *Universal History: the Oldest Historical Group of Nations and the Greeks*, ed. G. W. Prothero (New York: Harper & Brothers, 1885).
9. This book has been informed and made possible by my earlier Ph.D. study entitled *Narratives of Belonging in the Two Berlins: Kinship Formation and Nation-Building in the Context of the Cold War, 1945/49–1989*, Harvard University, 1989. It is scheduled for publication by Cambridge University Press.
10. See the discussion of "colonization of life-worlds" by Jürgen Habermas, *Theory of Communicative Action*, vol. II, trans. Thomas McCarthy (Boston: Beacon Press, 1987). Also see the

examination of increased use of "functional rationality" in the modern welfare state by K. U. Mayer and W. Mueller, "The State and the Structure of the Life Course," in eds. Sorensen, Weinert, and Sherrod, *Human Development and the Lifecourse* (Hillsdale, N. J.: Erlbaum, 1986); and the analysis of class distinctions in France by Pierre Bourdieu, *Distinction*, trans. Richard Nice (Cambridge: Harvard University Press, 1984).

11. See the discussion of "territorialization" in Giles Deleuze and Félix Guattari, *Anti-Oedipus: Capitalism and Schizophrenia*, trans. Robert Hurley, Mark Seem, and Helen R. Lane (New York: Viking Press, 1977); and see the analysis of commodification by Theodor Adorno and Max Horkheimer, *Dialectic of Enlightenment*, trans. John Cumming (New York: Seabury Press, 1972).

12. See the work of two anthropologists very much concerned with linking the personal and political, though doing so with quite different interests in mind: Clifford Geertz, *The Interpretation of Cultures* (New York: Basic Books, 1973), and Sally Falk Moore, *Social Facts and Fabrications: "Customary" Law on Kilimanjaro, 1880–1980* (Cambridge: Cambridge University Press, 1986).

Chapter 3

1. Edward Sapir, "Symbolism," *Encyclopedia of the Social Sciences XIV* (New York: The Macmillan Company, 1934, pp. 492–93).

2. Victor Turner, *Dramas, Fields, and Metaphors: Symbolic Action in Human Society* (Ithaca, N.Y.: Cornell University Press, 1966).

Chapter 4

1. See two of the most influential works in constructing a theory of totalitarianism: Carl Friedrich and Zbigniew Brzezinski, *Totalitarian Dictatorship and Autocracy* (Cambridge: Harvard University Press, 1965), and Hannah Arendt, *The Origins of Totalitarianism* (New York: Harcourt Brace Jovanovich, 1951).

2. Claude Lévi-Strauss, *The Savage Mind*, trans. Rodney Needham (Chicago: University of Chicago Press, 1966).
3. Walter Benjamin, *Reflections*, ed. Edmund Jephcott (New York: Harcourt Brace Jovanovich, 1978).
4. See the analyses by Rainer Land, "Die Grenze ist offen," in *Aufbruch in eine DDR*, ed. Hubertus Knabe (Hamburg: Rowohlt, 1989) and Michael Brie and Rainer Land, "Aspekte der Krise," *Einheit* 12/89.
5. For an analysis of the *Kleinbürger* in German culture, see Bertold Franke, *Die Kleinbürger. Begriff, Ideologie, Politik* (Frankfurt: Campus Verlag, 1988).

Chapter 8

1. Scott Long, "Useful Laughter: Camp and Seriousness," *Southwest Review* 74:1 (Winter 1989).

Chapter 9

1. Much of this is drawn from the superb analysis of these movements by Liisa Malkki, *The Origin of a Device of Power: The Refugee Camp in Post-war Europe*, unpubl. manuscript, 1985. For an examination of the role of territoriality in German identity formation, see John Borneman, *State, Territory, and Identity Formation in the Postwar Berlins*, 1945–1989, unpubl. manuscript, 1989.

Chapter 10

1. Stanley Aronowitz, "The Future of Socialism," *Social Text* 24 (1990).